COLOR

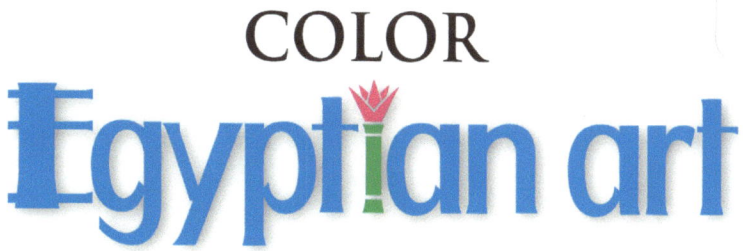

Egyptian art

Conceived, Designed, and Illustrated by:

Mrinal Mitra

Series Edited by:

Swarna Mitra & Malika Mitra

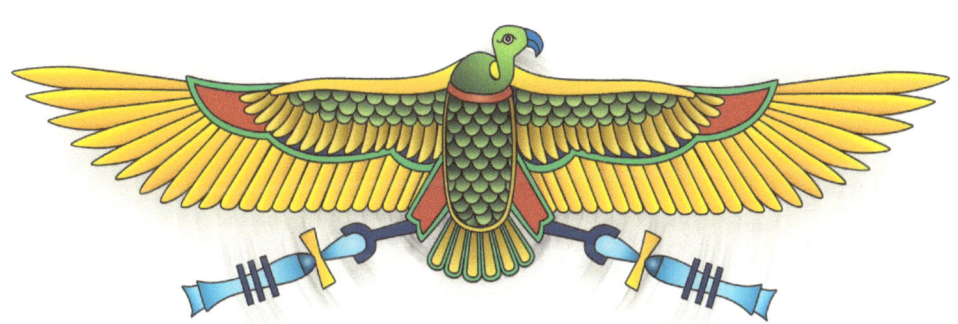

WORLD CULTURE COLORING SERIES

This series is dedicated to the citizens of the world;
from the young blooming minds of children, to the aspired individuals of all ages.

A Quail Chick

Man, Son

Sail Upstream

Egyptian Hieroglyphs

Hieroglyphics were everywhere in ancient Egypt. They were constituted their language for over 3000 years. Hieroglyphics may have begun in prehistoric era as pictorial writing. Early Egyptians devised a rebus to spell the desired word. For example: picture of a bee plus a leaf to show the English word 'belief' in written language.

About 700 hieroglyphs commonly used during the New Kingdom, at least 100 remained strictly visual.

Cattle, Ox

Bee, Honey

Goose

Color the drawings above using your preferred choice of colors.

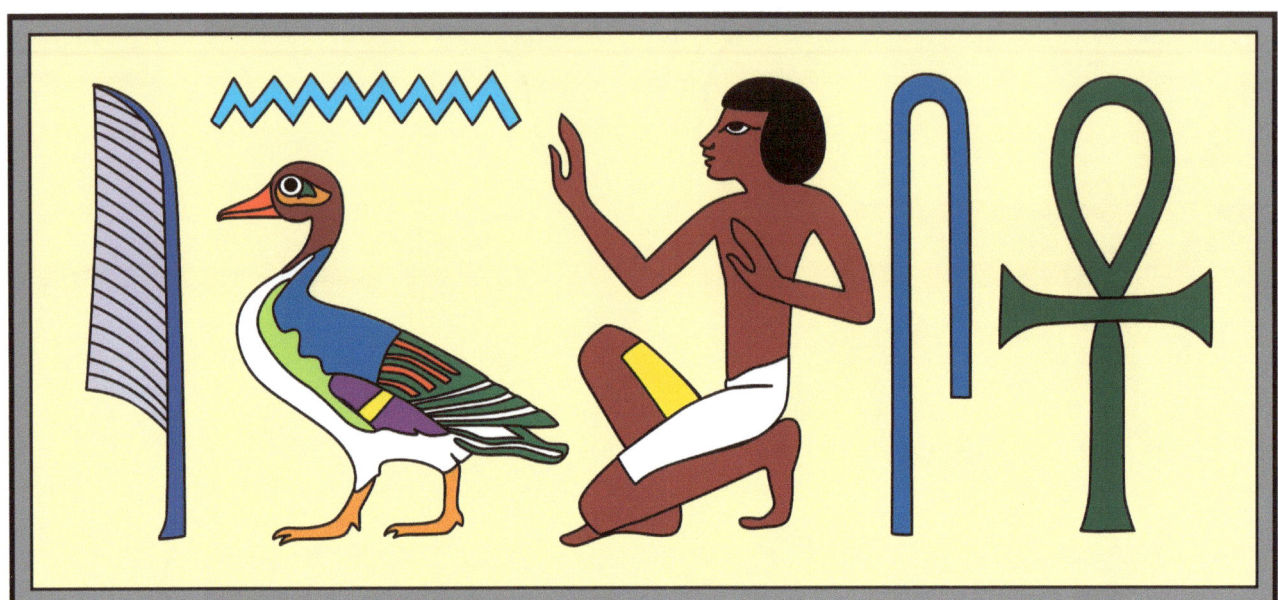

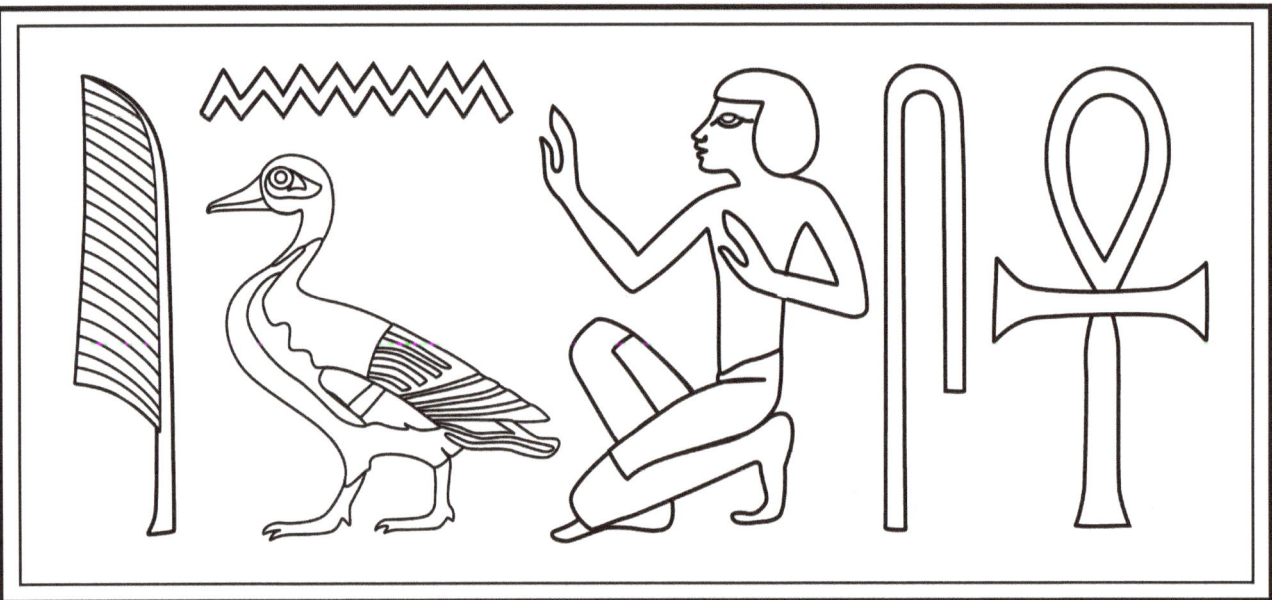

A Father's tribute to his son.
"It is my son who causes my name to live upon this stela."

Animals and Birds on a slate palette.
The late Predynastic period 3150 B.C.E.

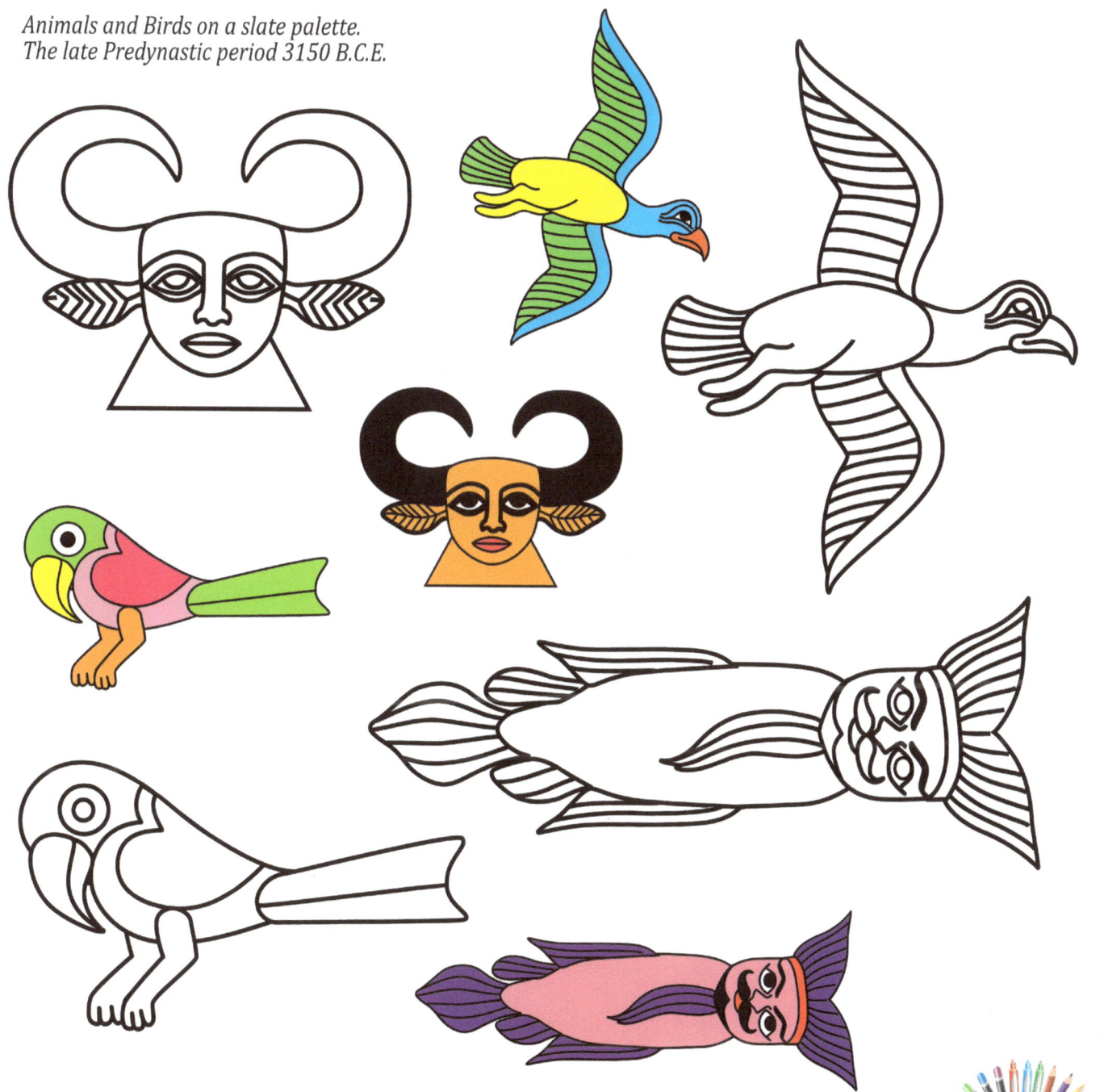

Color the drawings above using your preferred choice of colors.

5

From a panel painting; sometime in 14th Century B.C.E., describing harvest being carried away by farmers.

Color the drawings above using your preferred choice of colors.

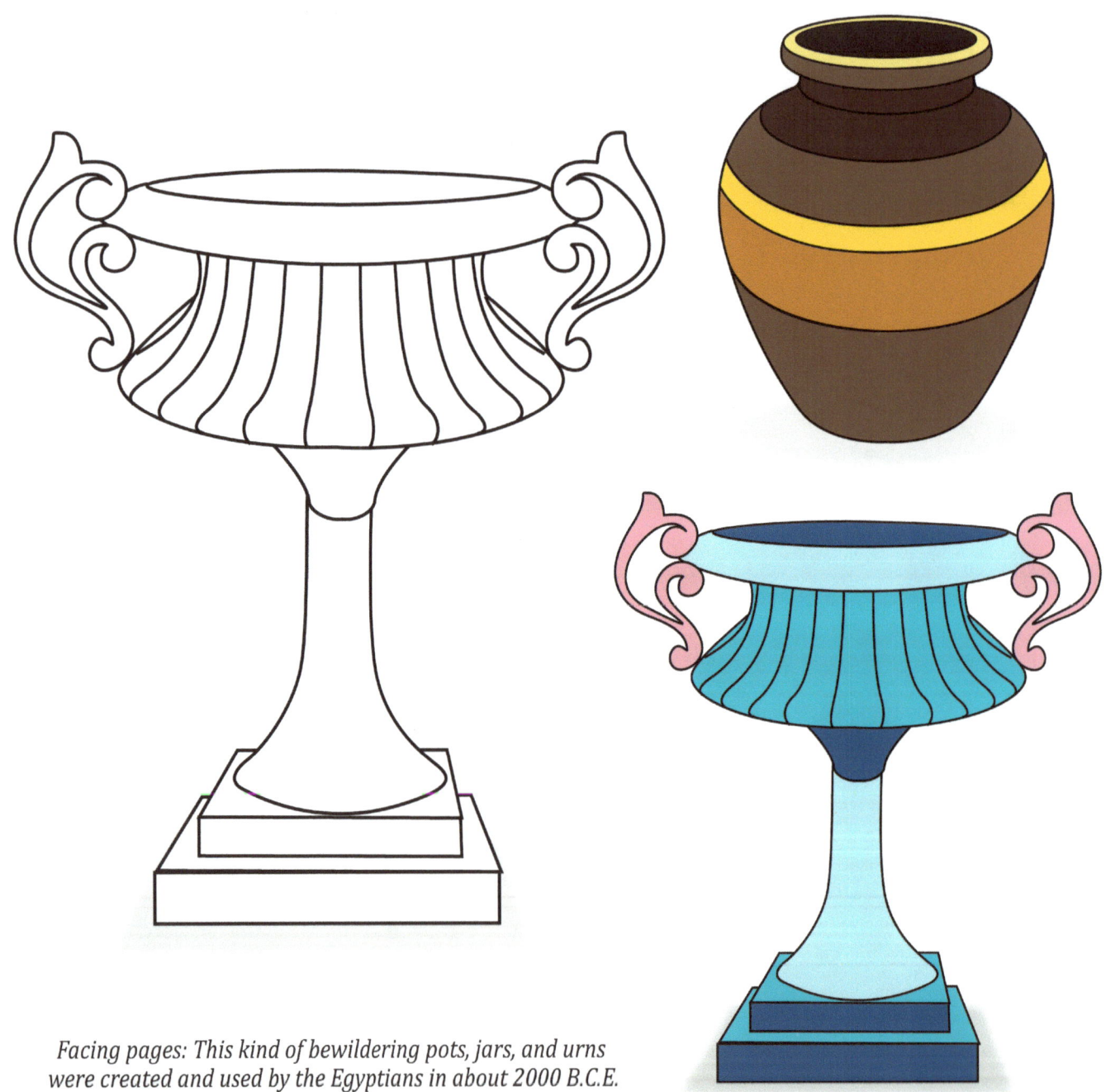

Facing pages: This kind of bewildering pots, jars, and urns were created and used by the Egyptians in about 2000 B.C.E.

Color the drawings above using your preferred choice of colors.

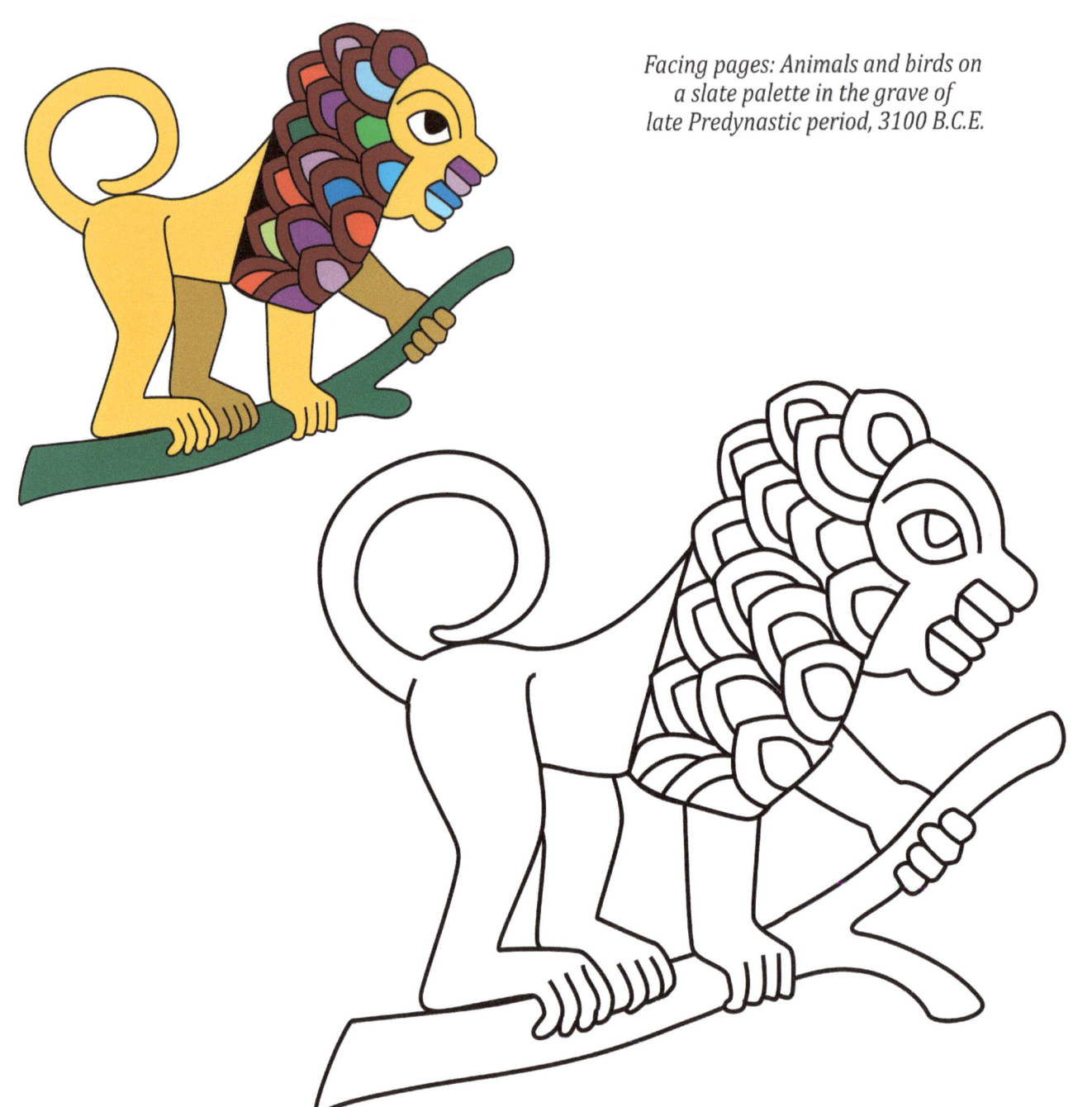

*Facing pages: Animals and birds on
a slate palette in the grave of
late Predynastic period, 3100 B.C.E.*

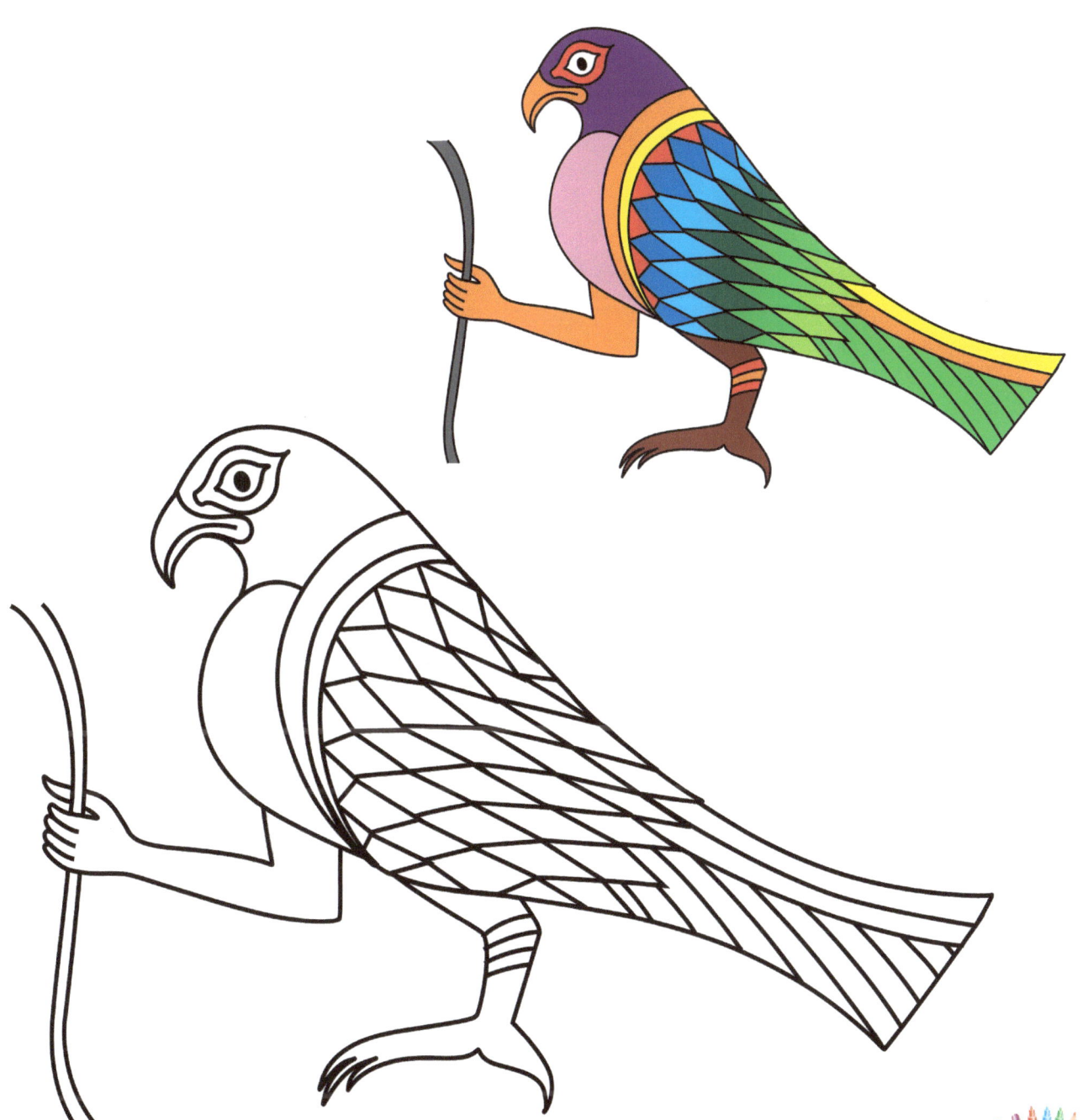

Color the drawings above using your preferred choice of colors.

From a panel painting sometime in
14th Century B.C.E., describing harvest being transported by boat.

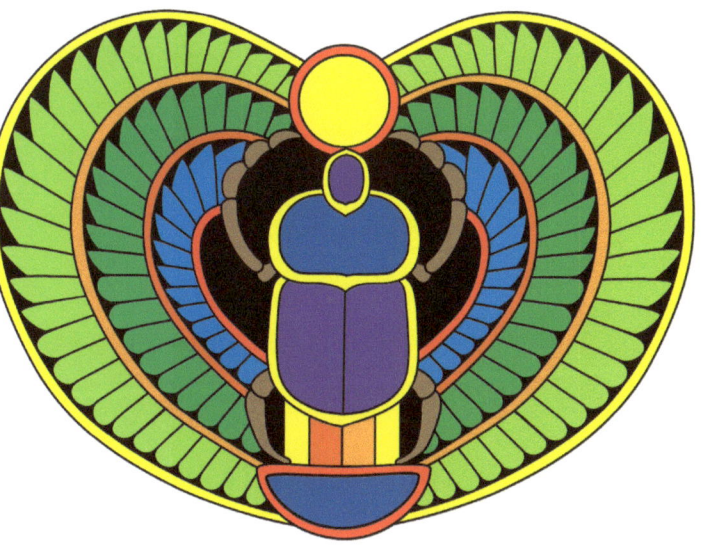

Jewelry, bearing scarab.
Many similar ornaments found
in Tutankhamun's tomb. 1332 - 1323 B.C.E.

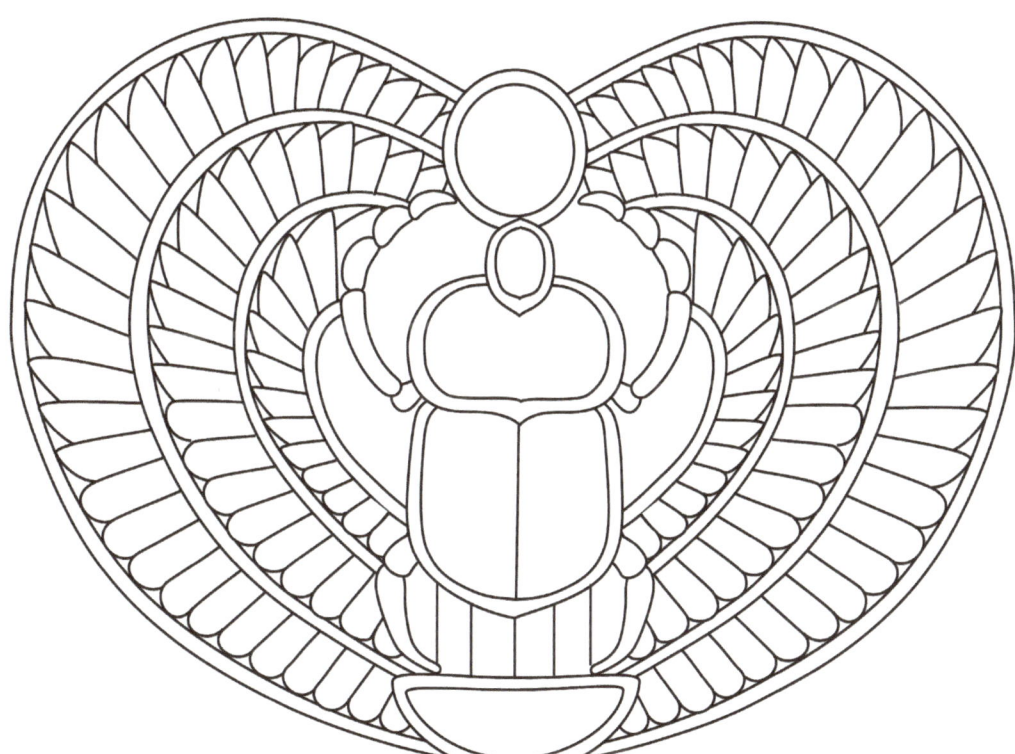

Color the drawings above using your preferred choice of colors.

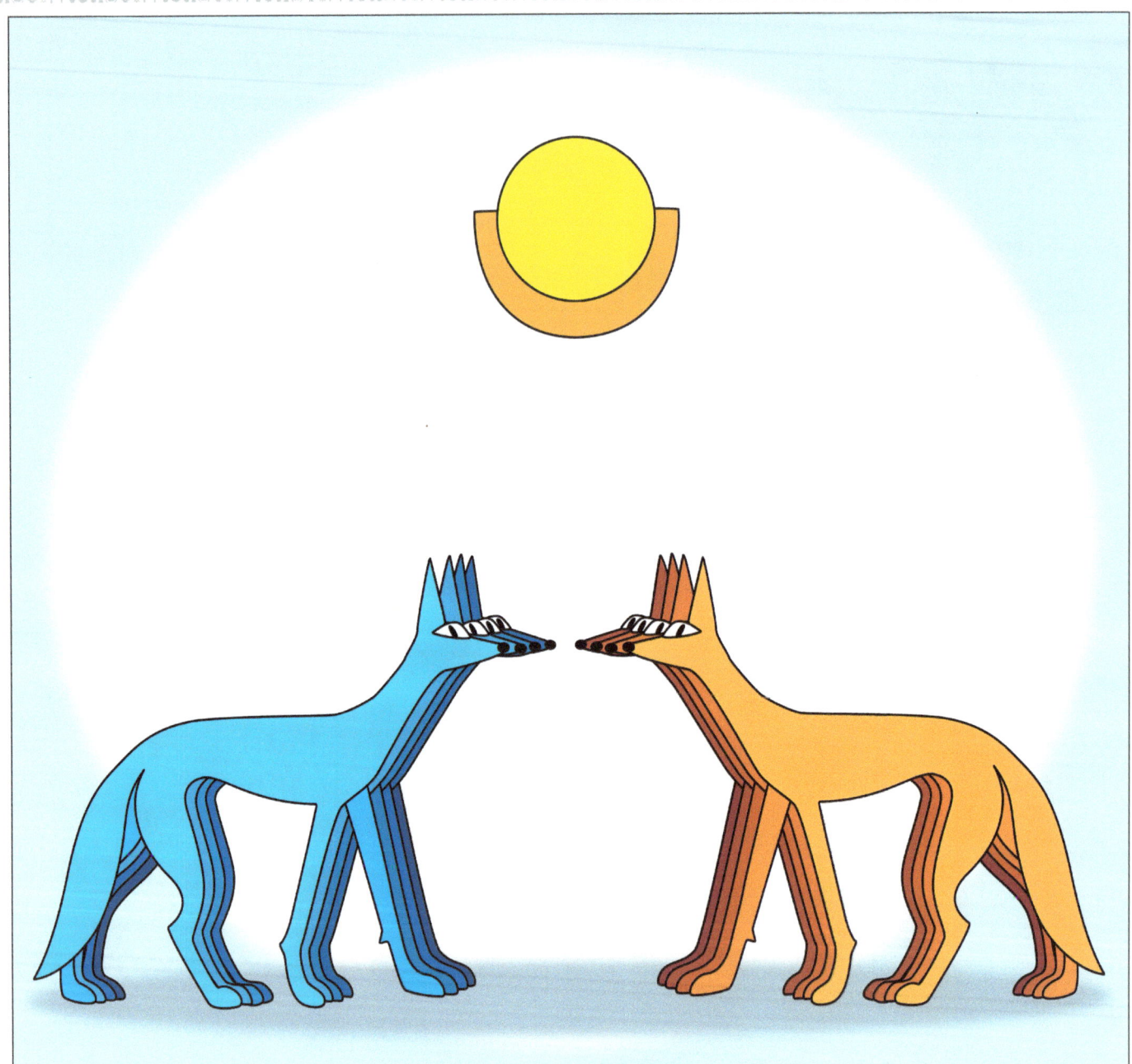

Jackals in a row from an Egyptian painting in the temple. On top placed Egyptian Sun disc. Circa 2000 B.C.E.

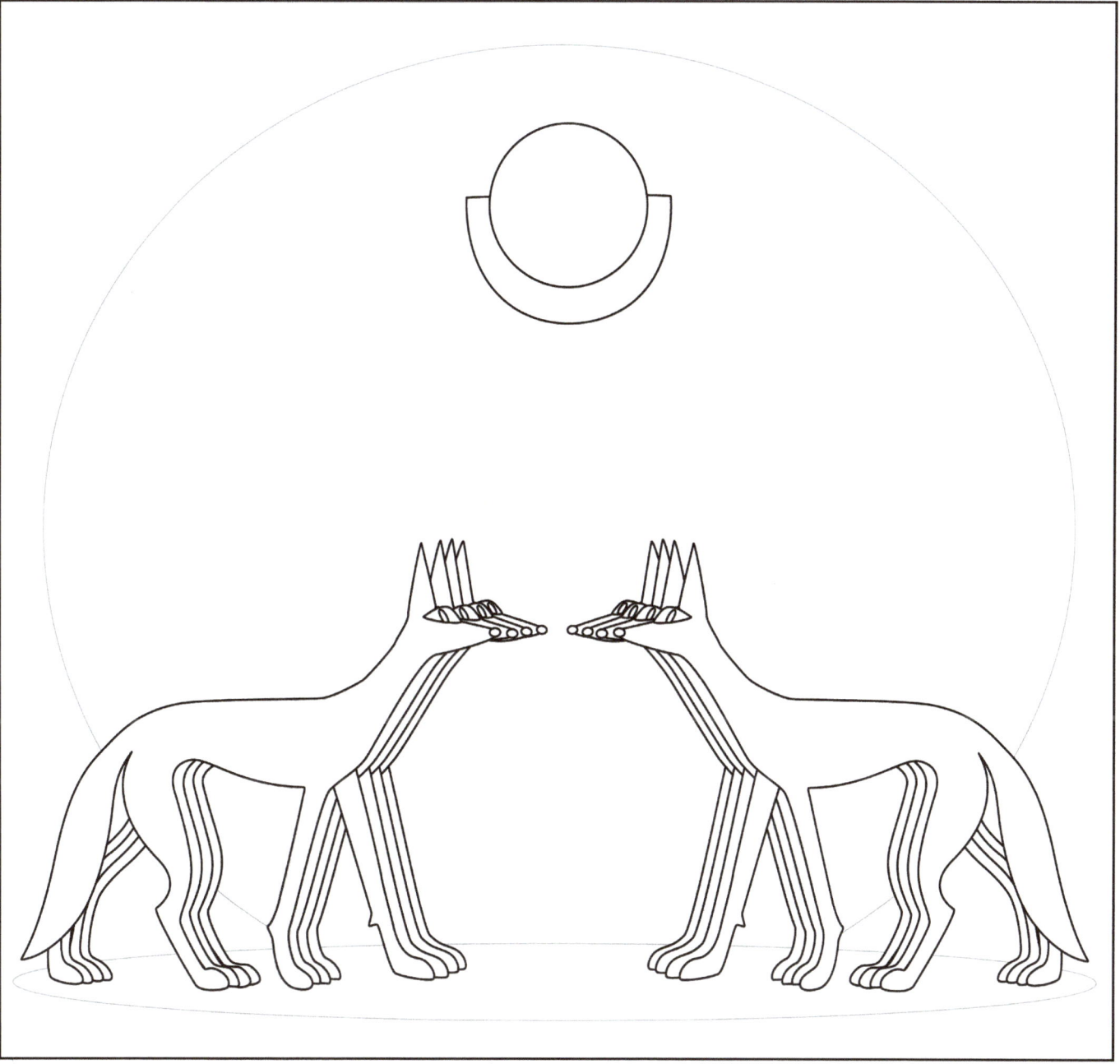

Color the drawing above using your preferred choice of colors.

On relief work in Saqqara, tomb of Meraruka; Old Kingdom.
Sixth Dynasty, 2330 B.C.E. An agricultural worker carrying water containers.

Color the drawing above using your preferred choice of colors.

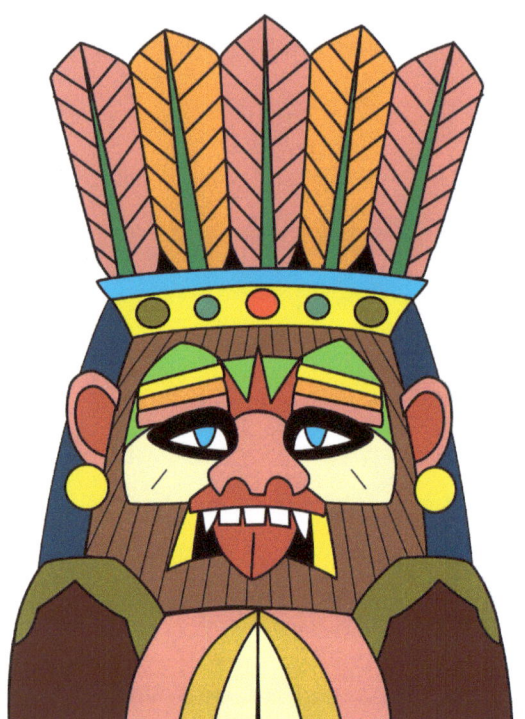

BES

*A lion-headed dwarf,
scared off the evil spirits.*

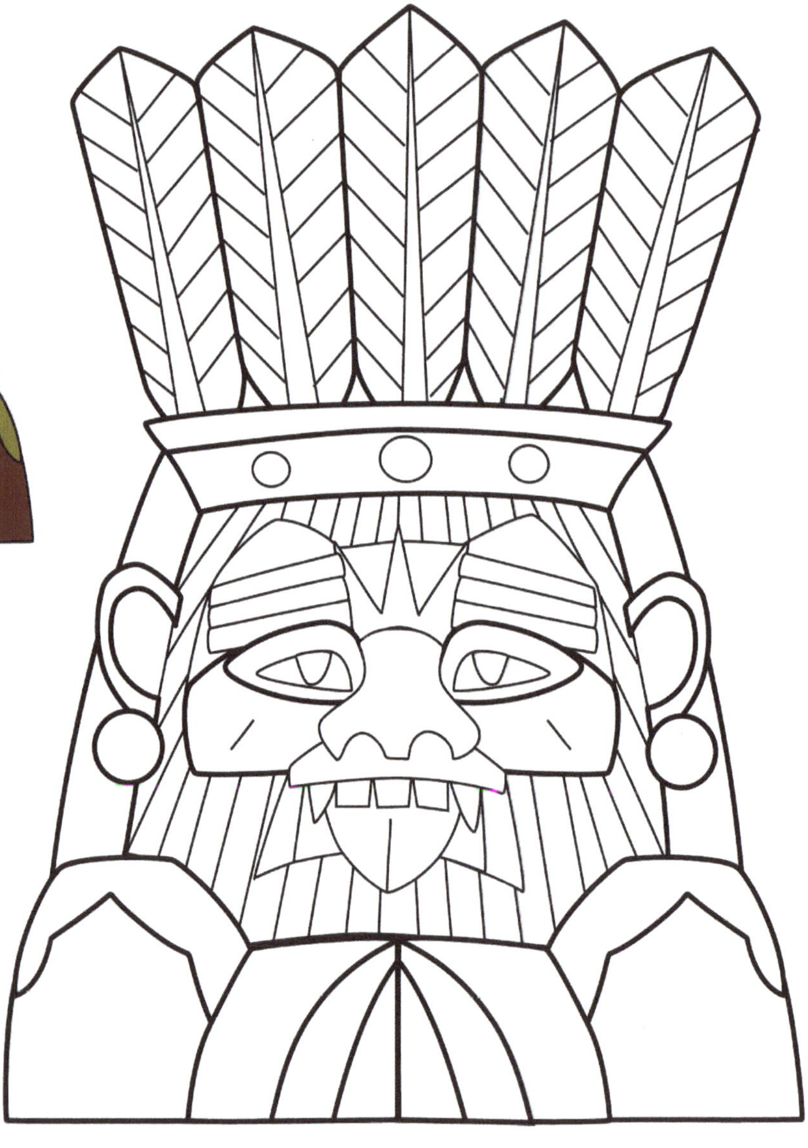

Egyptian Art

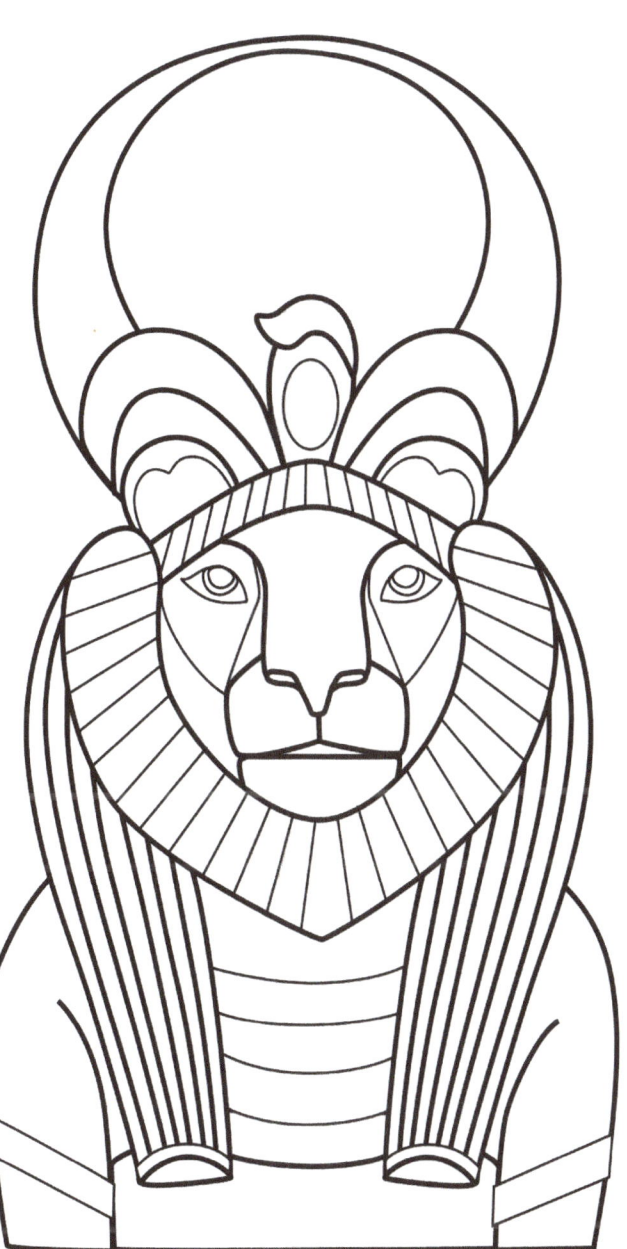

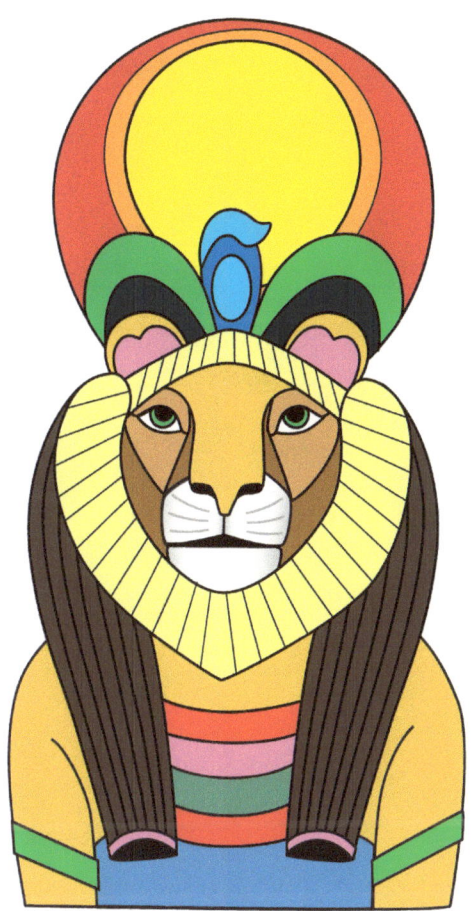

SEKHMET

War goddess- a part woman and part lioness.

Color the drawings above using your preferred choice of colors.

19

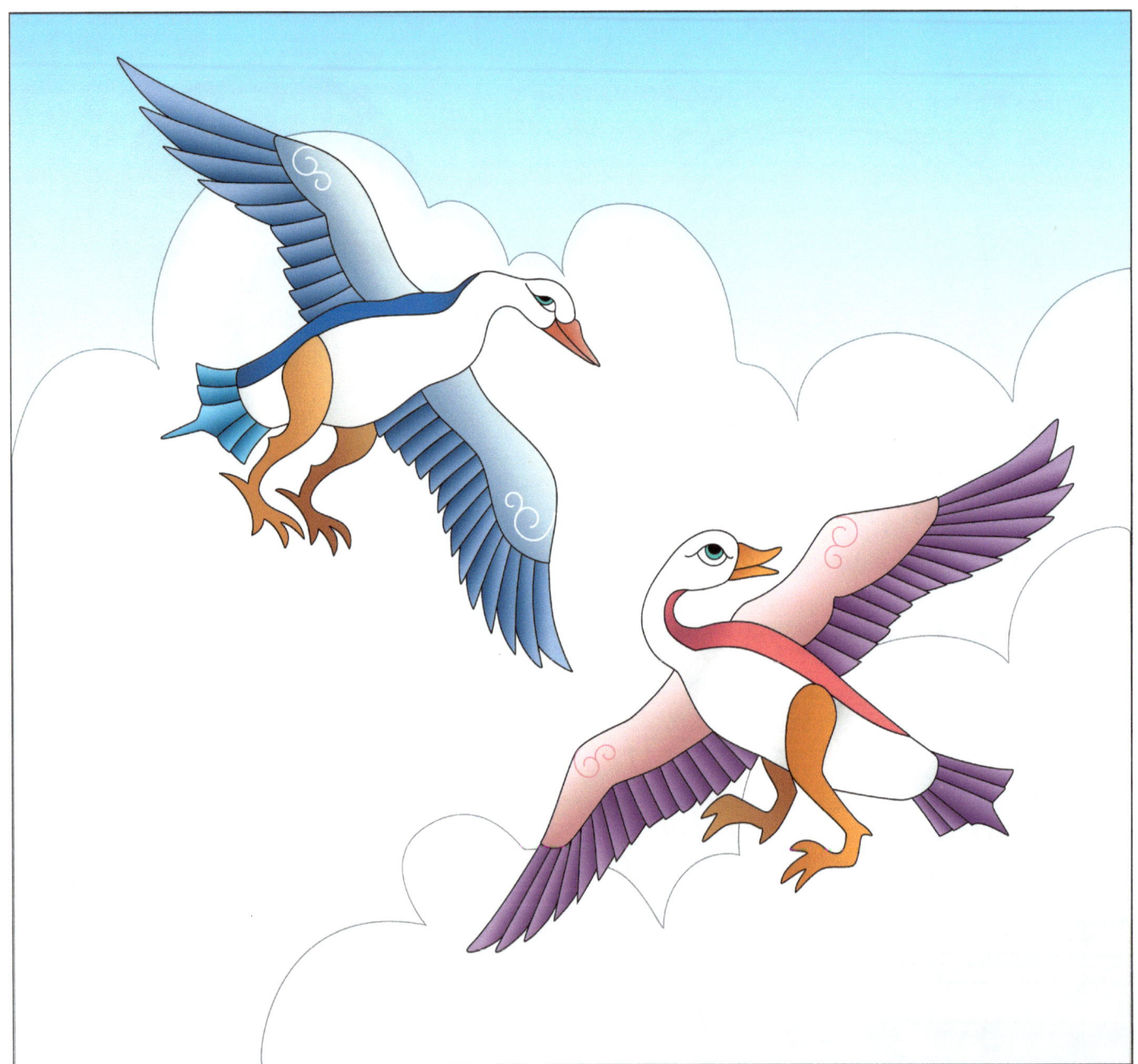

Flying birds from painting on stucco. The New Kingdom,
Eighteenth Dynasty, 1400 B.C.E. From the tomb of Nebamun at Thebes.

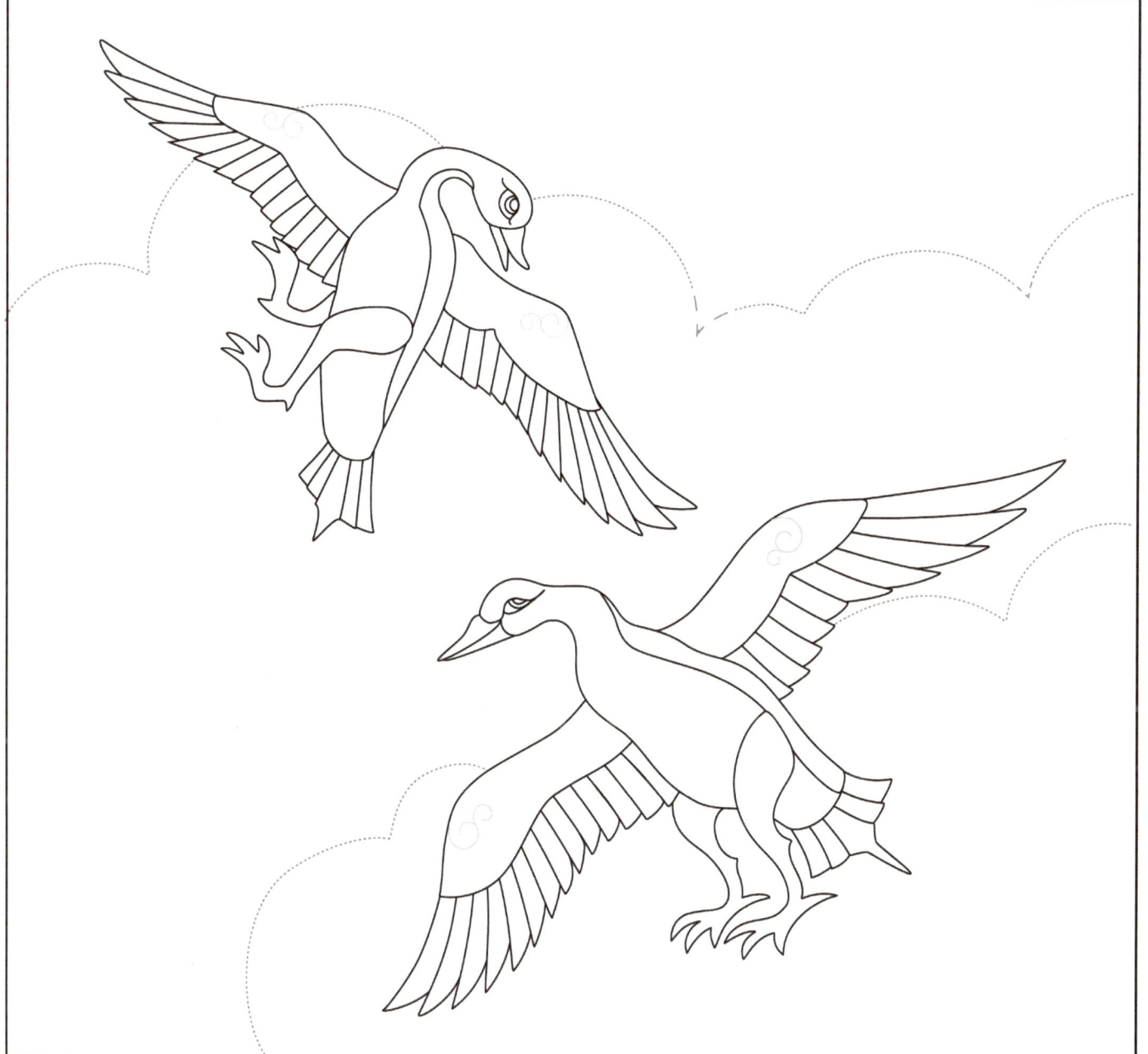

Color the drawing above using your preferred choice of colors.

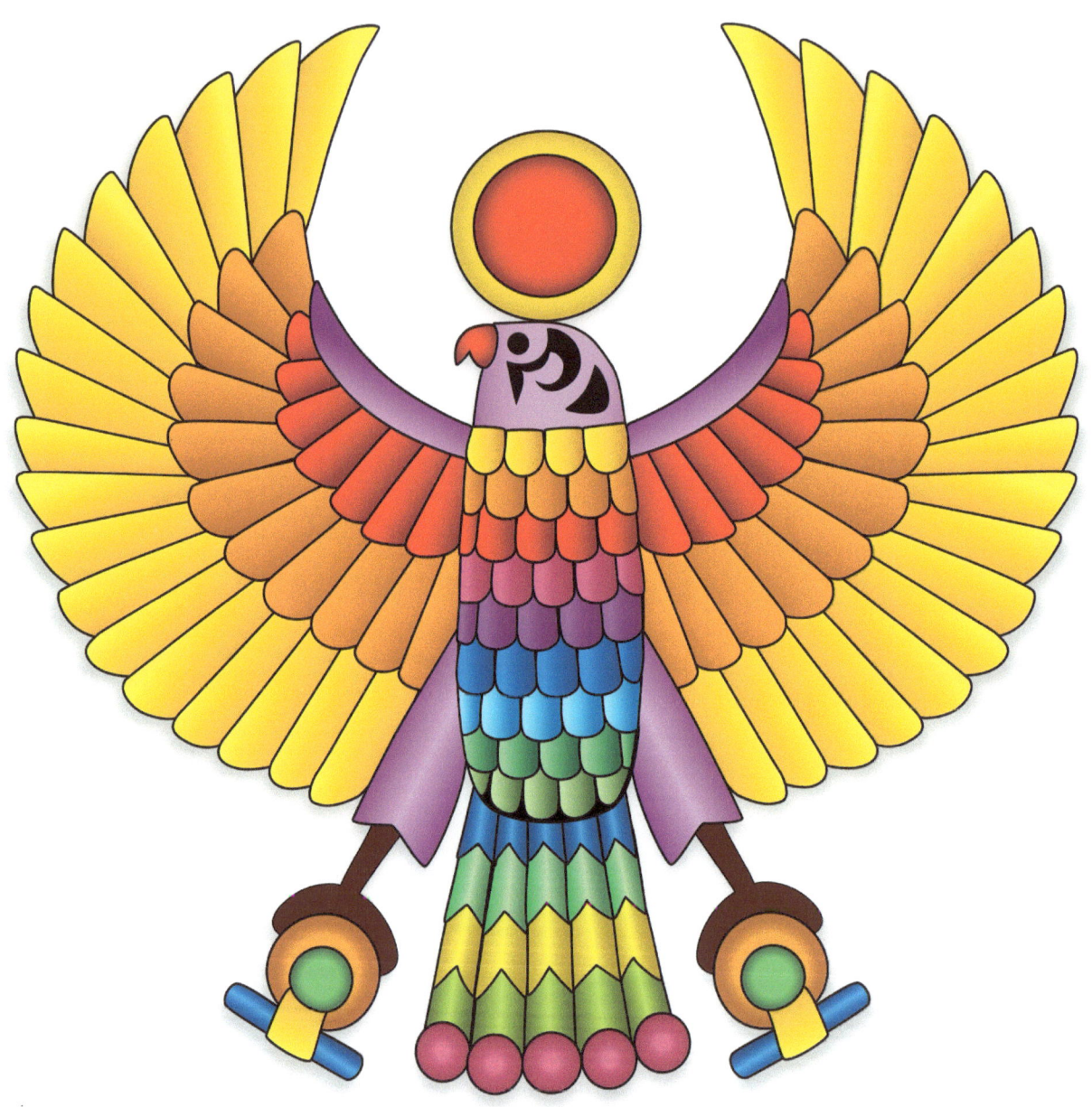

Falcon Pendant.
During Tutankhamun's reign. 1332 - 1323 B.C.E.

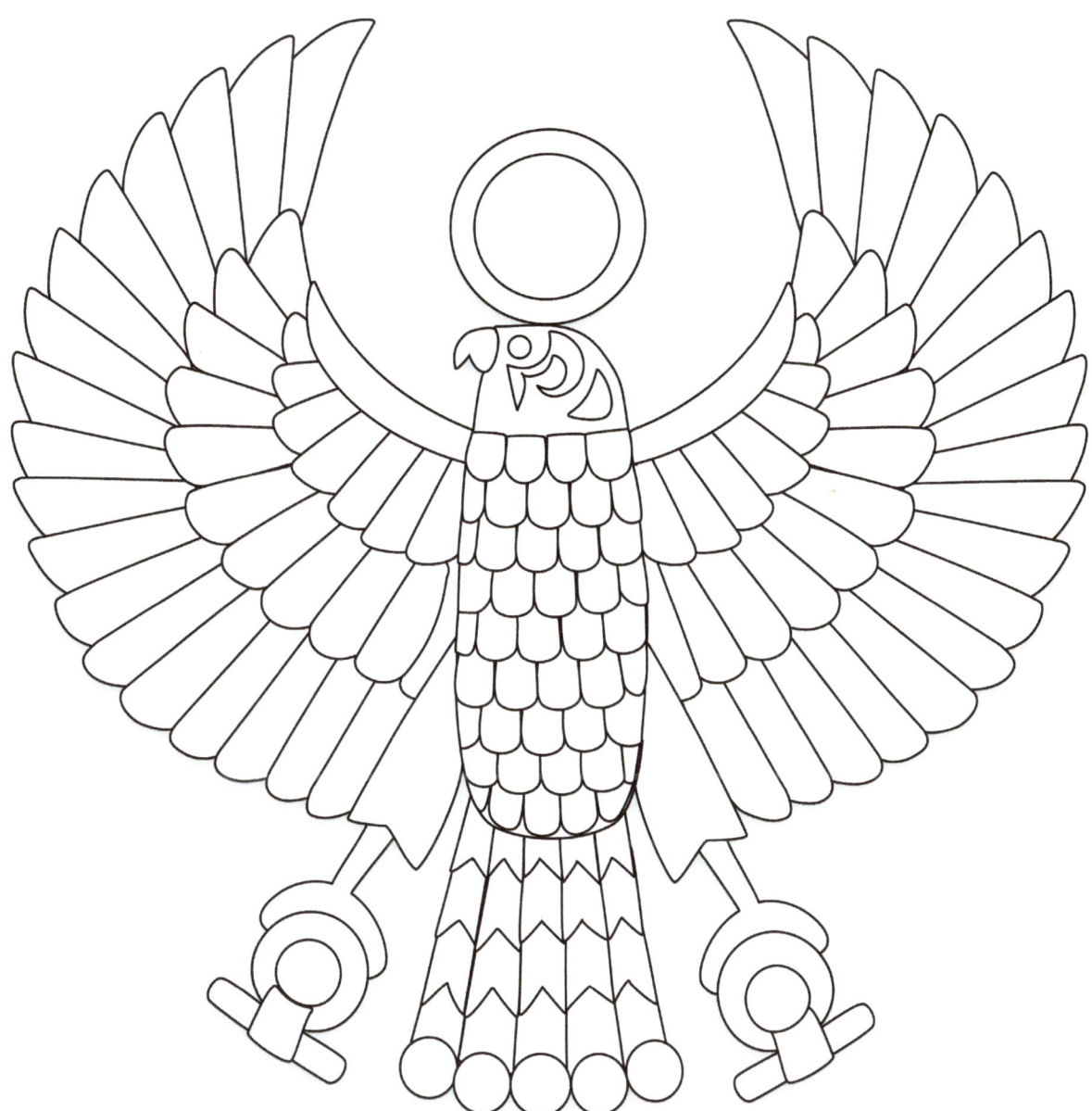

Color the drawing above using your preferred choice of colors.

23

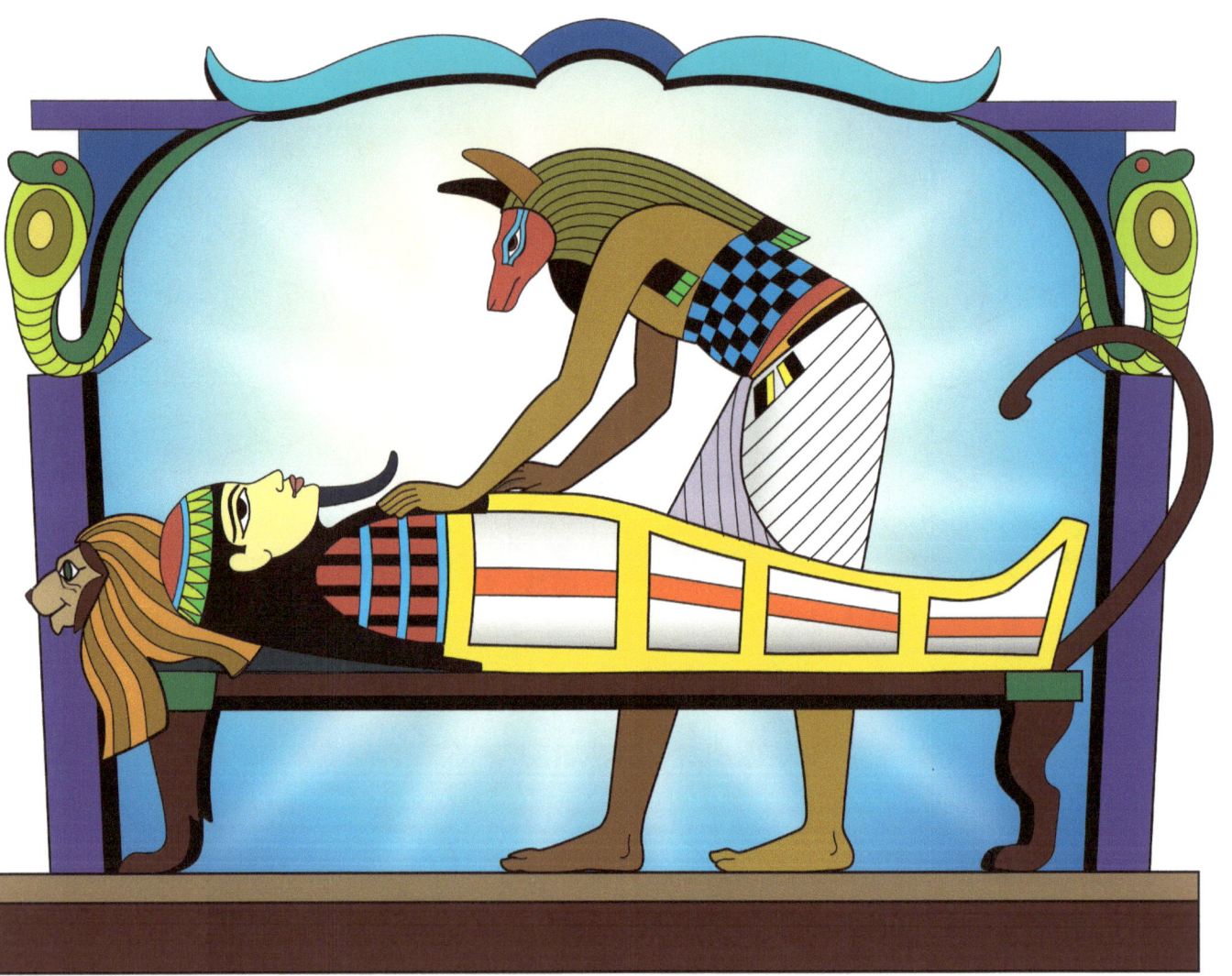

*The body of a deceased man is embalmed and prepared
for the tomb by Anubis, the protector of the dead. The body is lying on a lion-headed bier.*

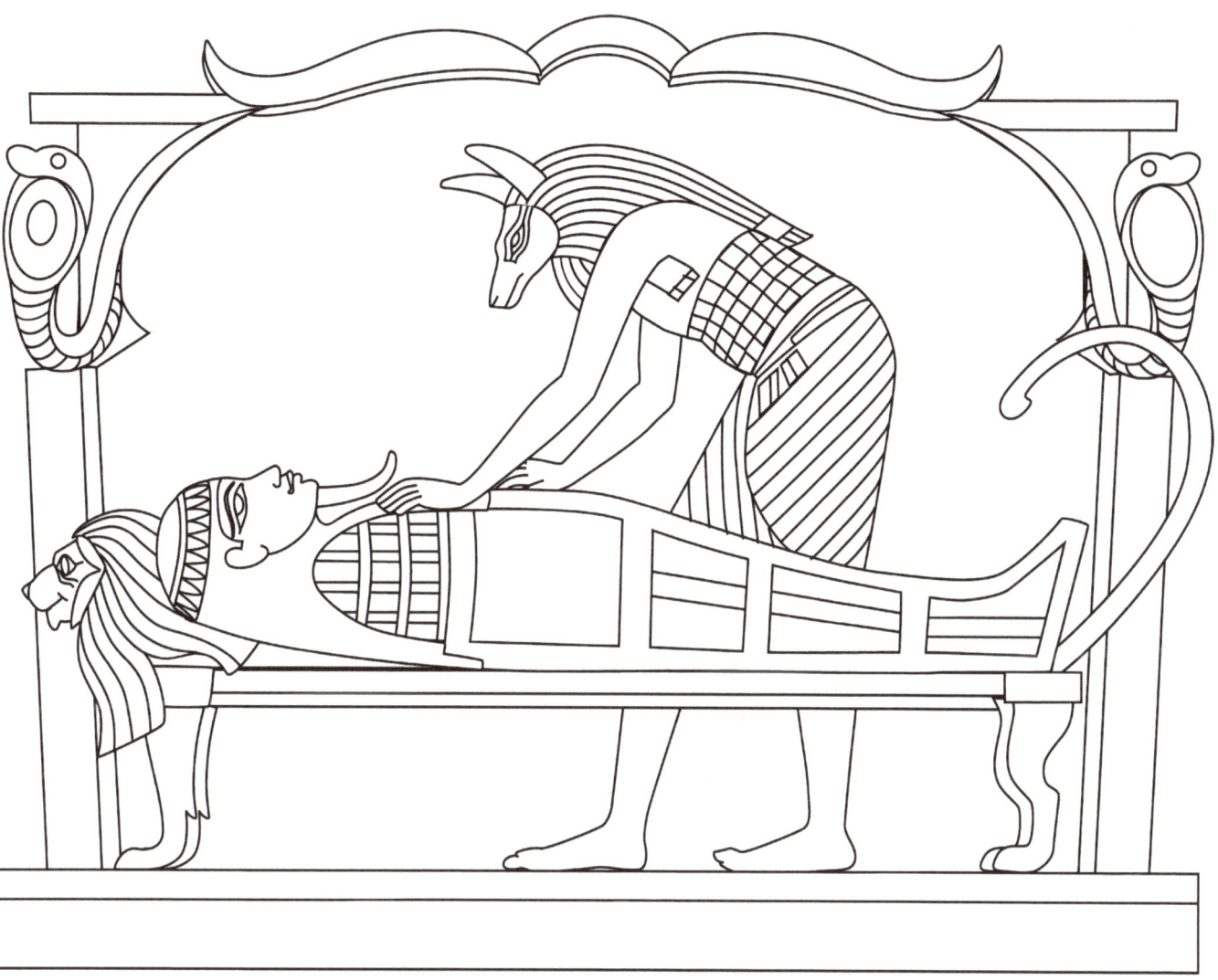

Color the drawing above using your preferred choice of colors.

25

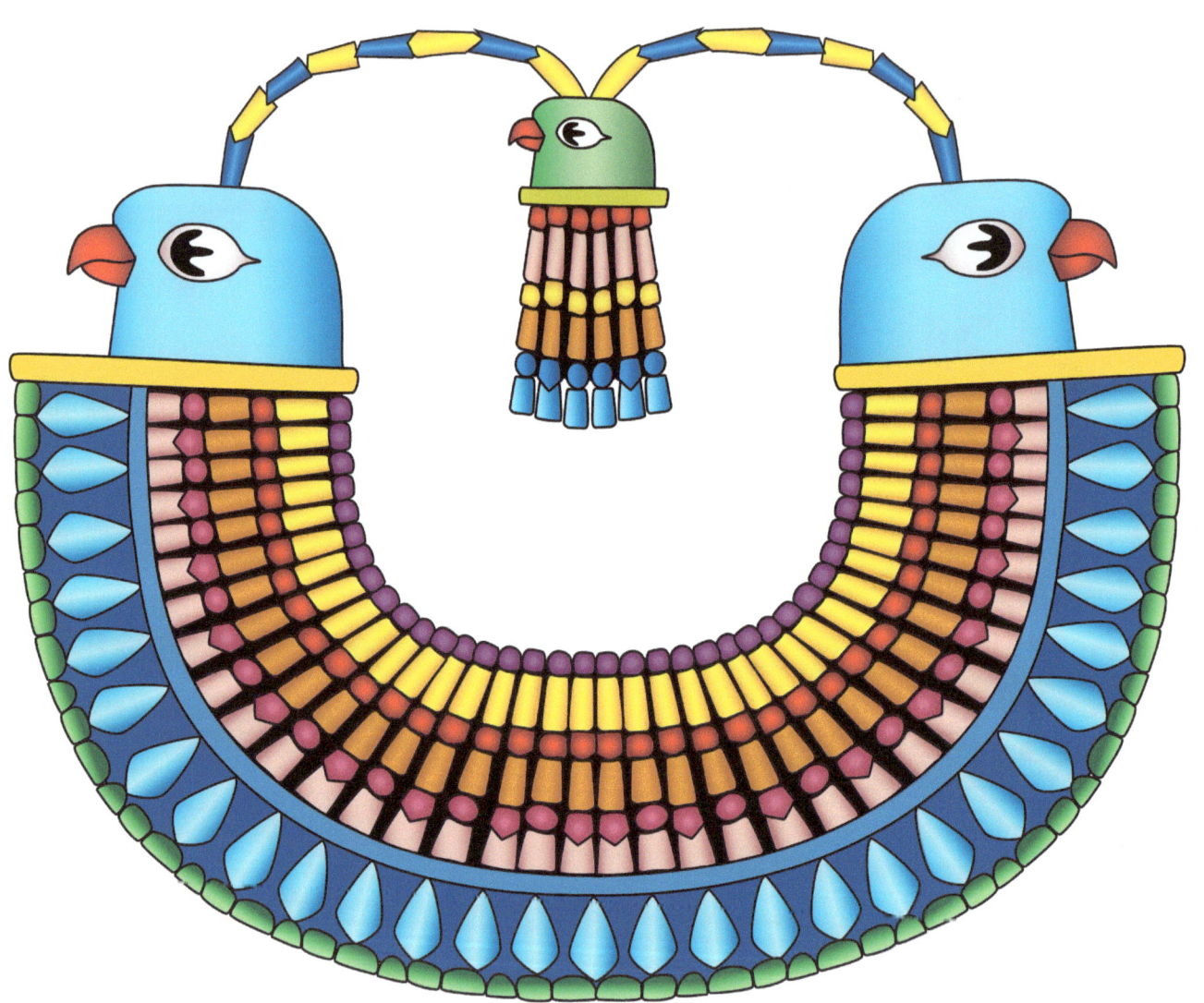

*A necklace with the falcon head on both sides. The beads
are made of glass, calcite, lapis lazuli, and electrum.
In the centre, is a counter-weight, used at the back
of heavy necklace to keep them in place.
Found in Tutankhamun's tomb. 1332 - 1323 B.C.E.*

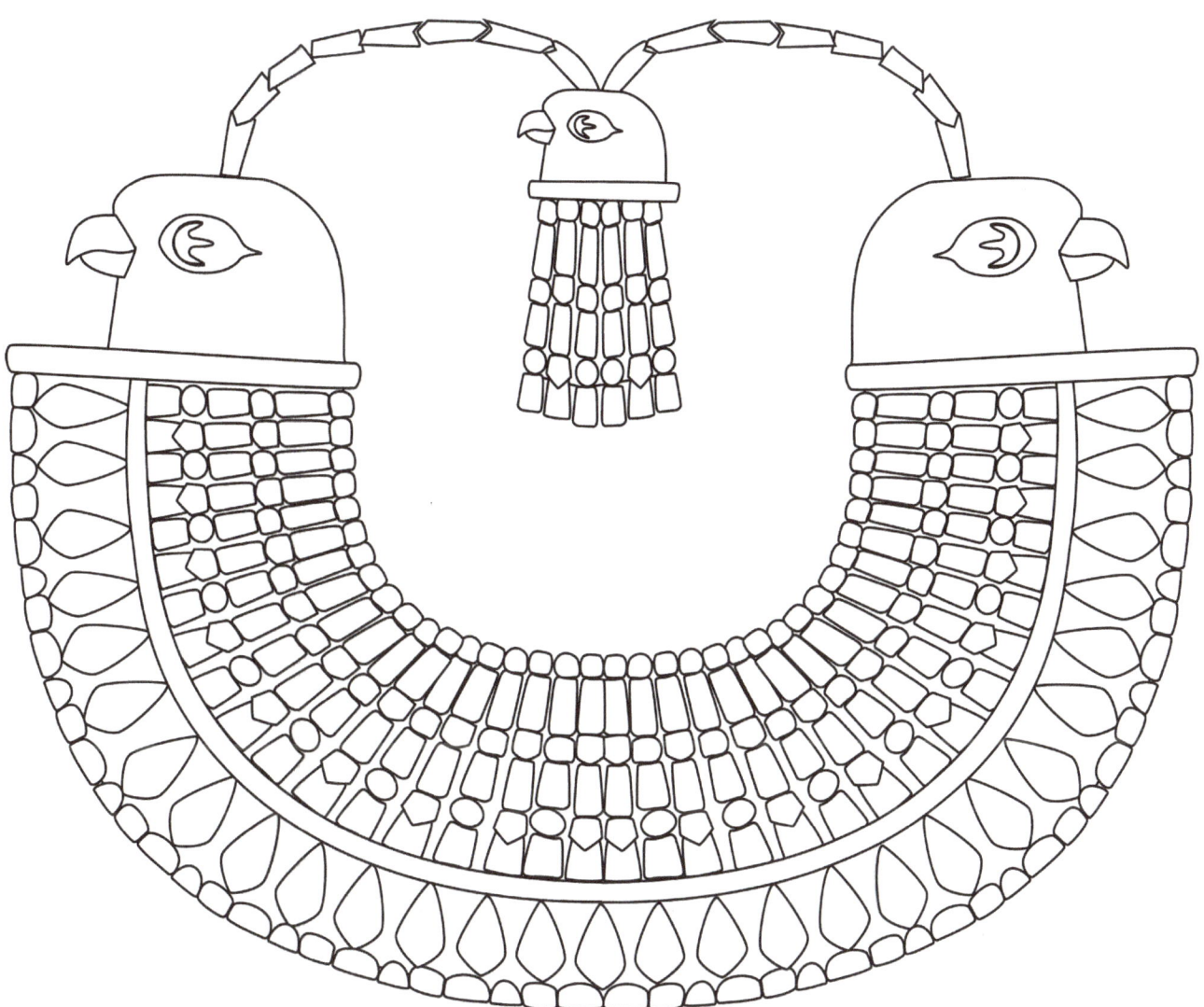

Color the drawing above using your preferred choice of colors.

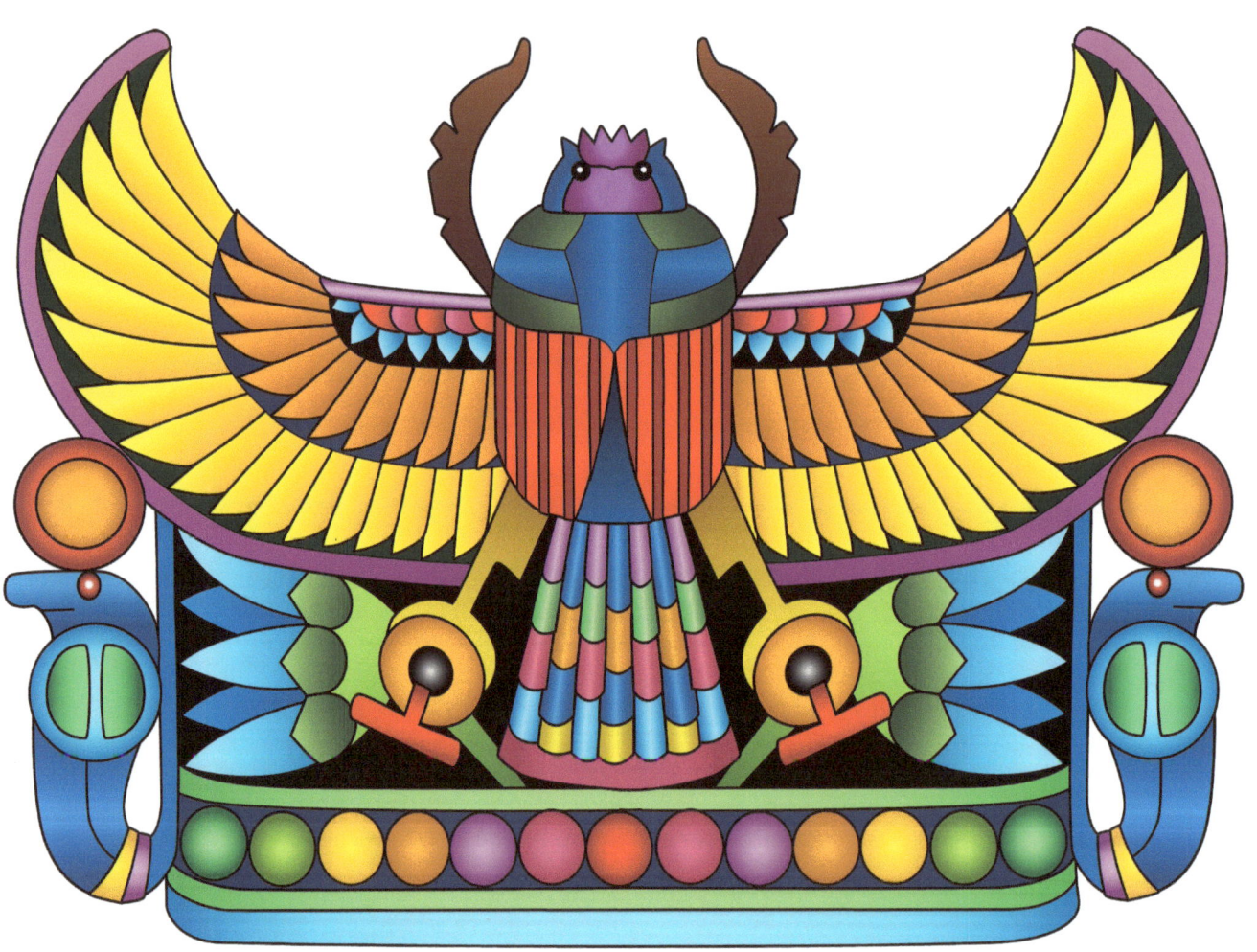

Jewelry bearing scarab. Many similar ornaments found in Tutankhamun's tomb. 1332 - 1323 B.C.E.

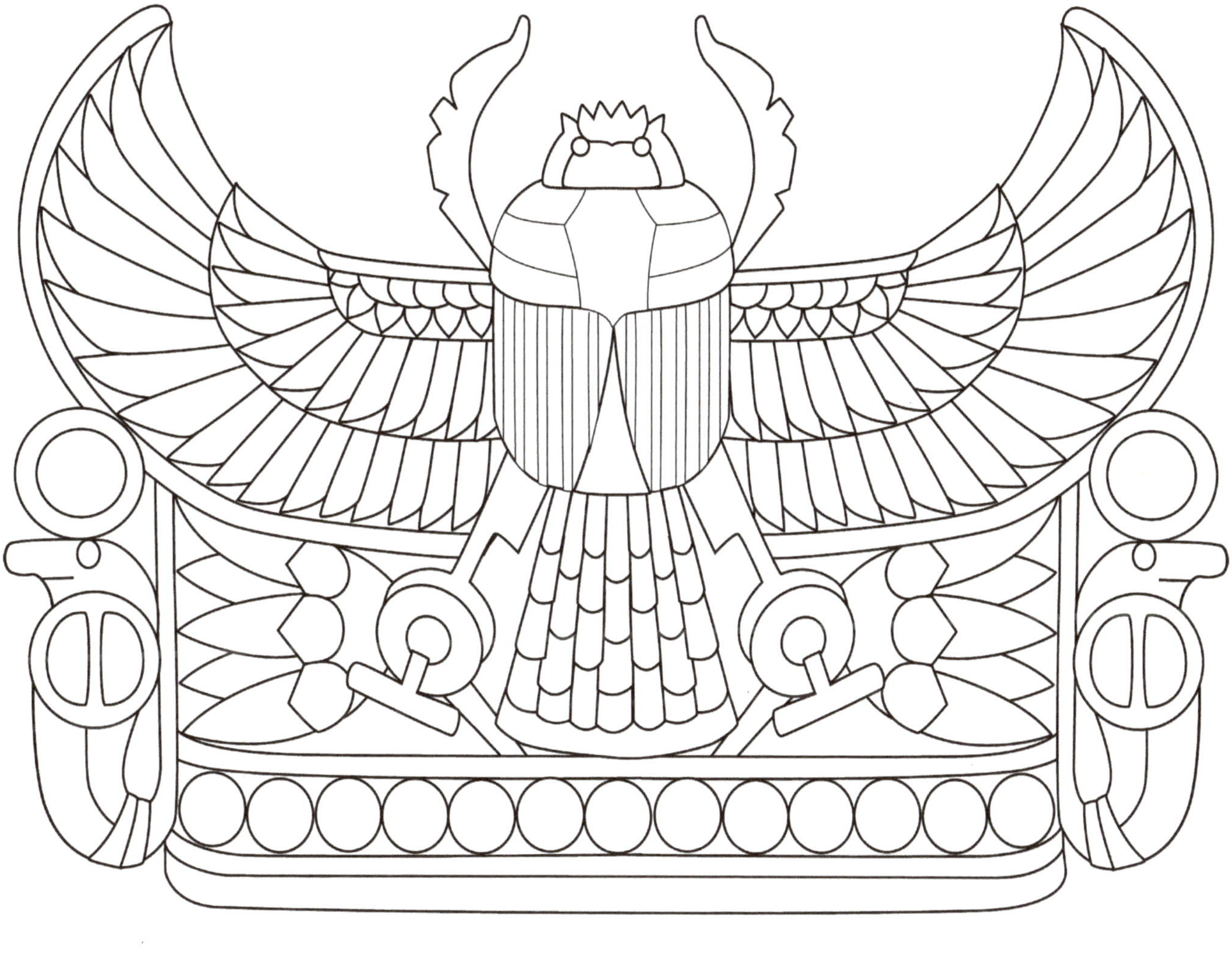

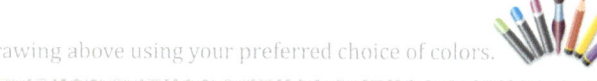

Color the drawing above using your preferred choice of colors.

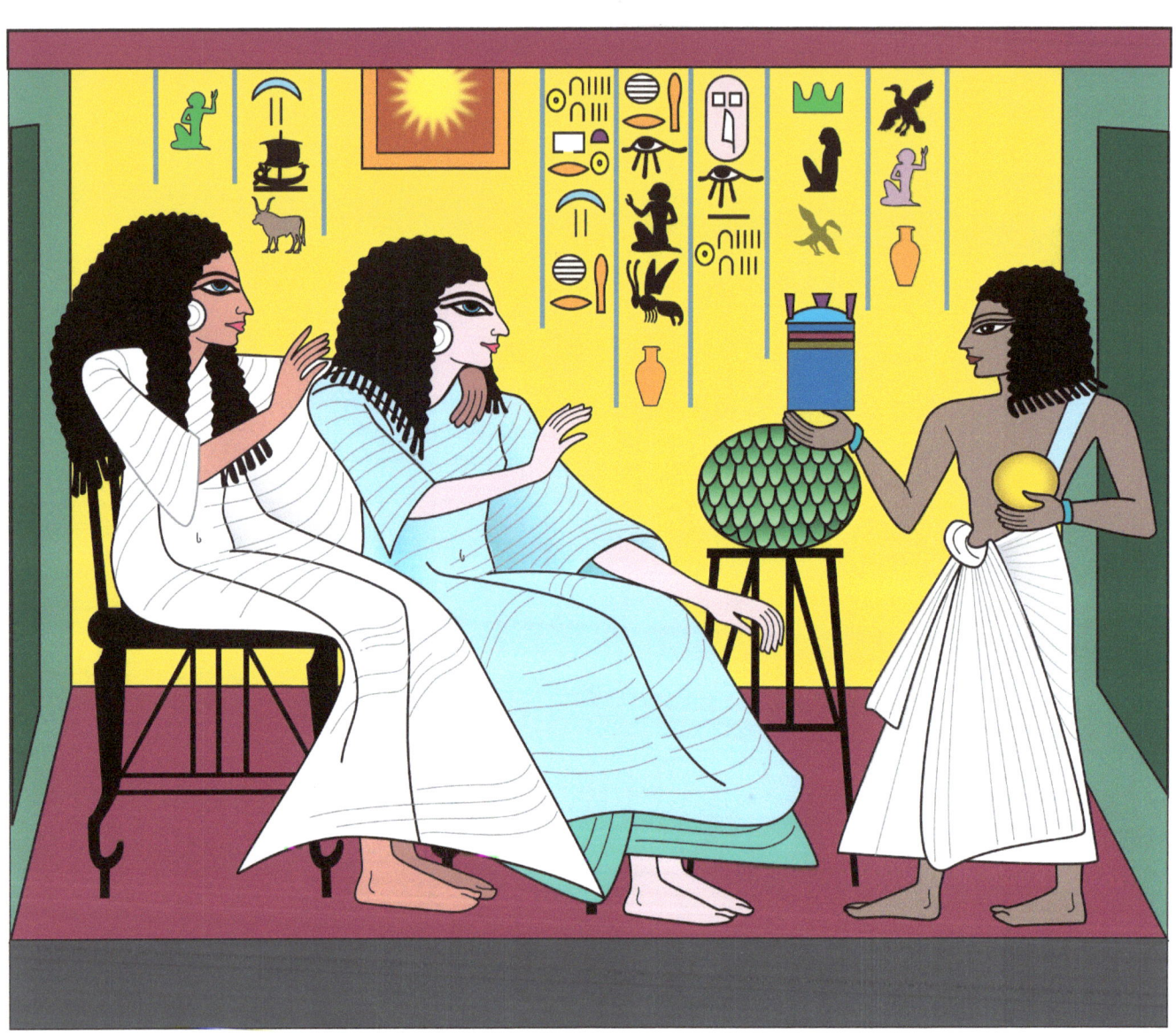

From an ancient tomb painting showing a bereaved family. A departed official's son offering votive gifts.

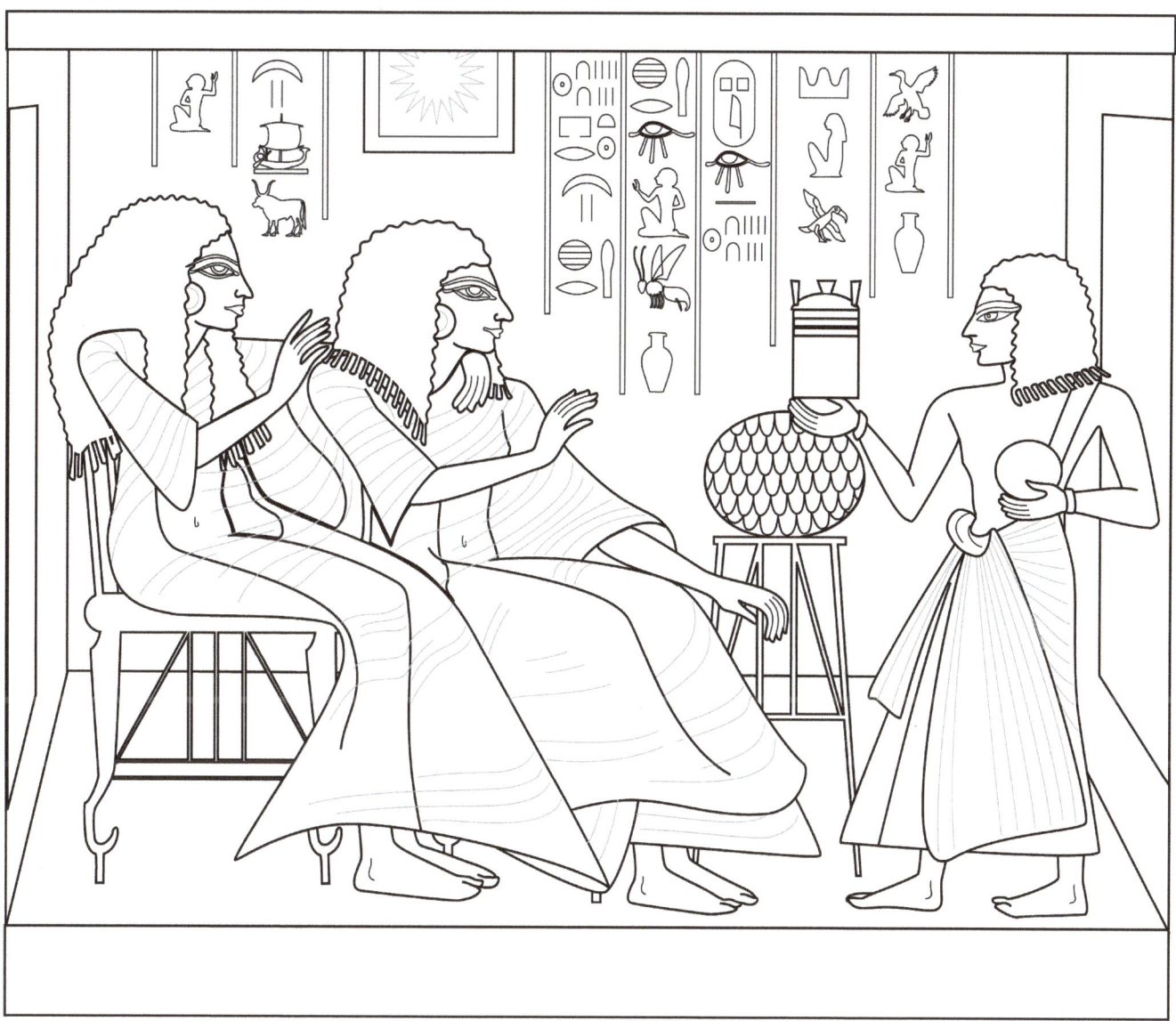

Color the drawing above using your preferred choice of colors.

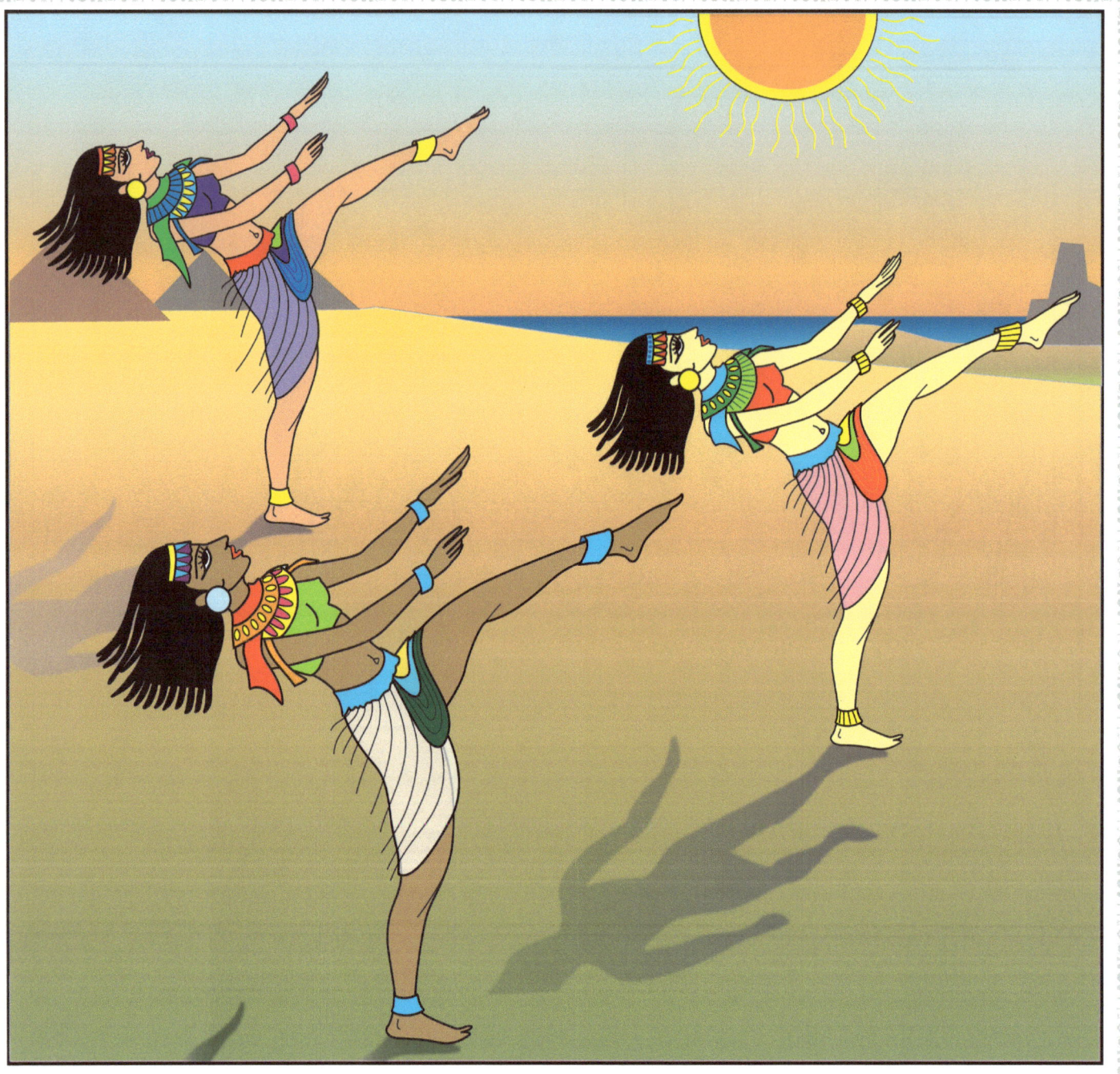

Dancing girls. Painted on plaster. Thebes, Eighteenth Dynasty, Circa 1425 B.C.E.

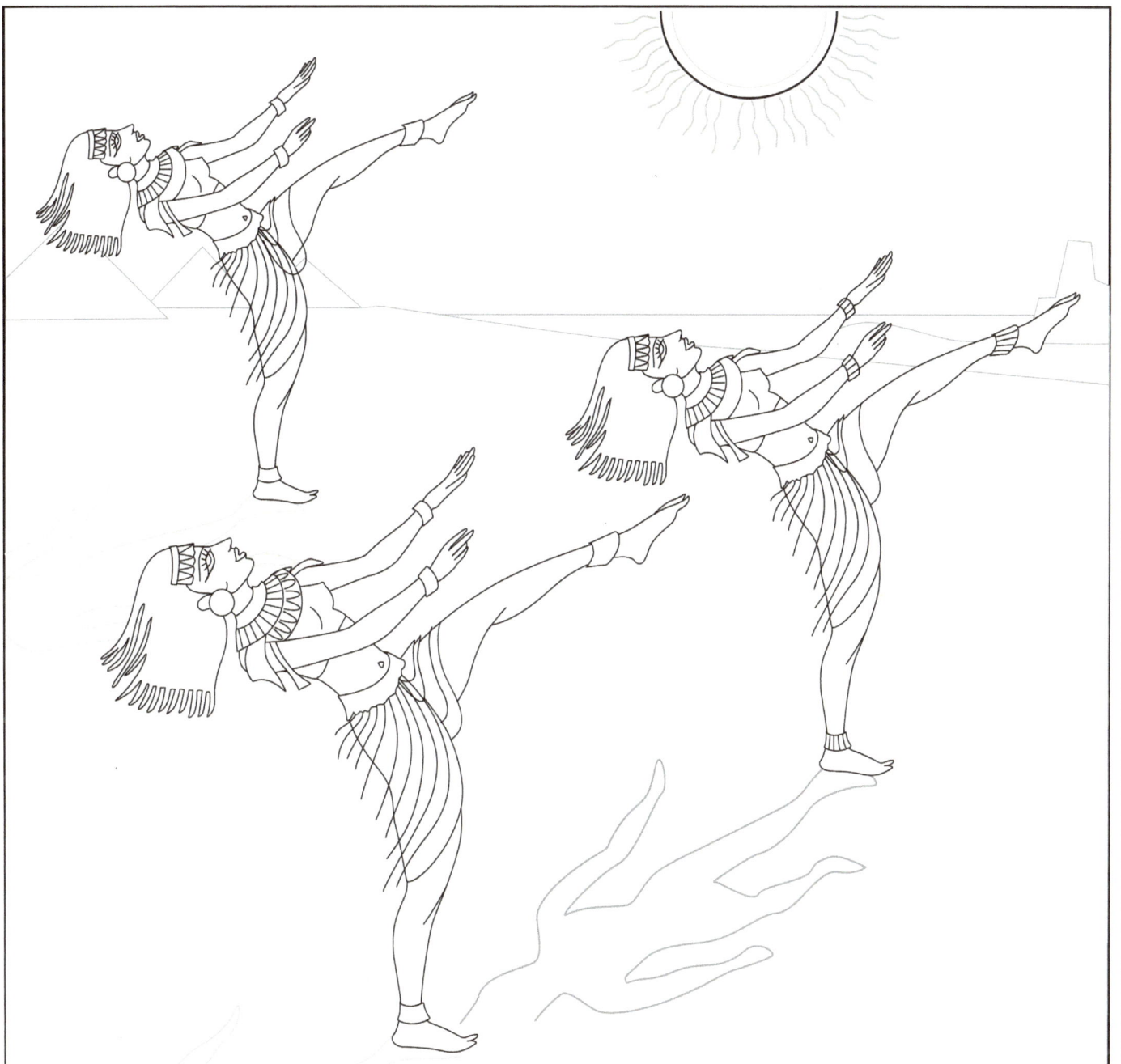

Color the drawing above using your preferred choice of colors.

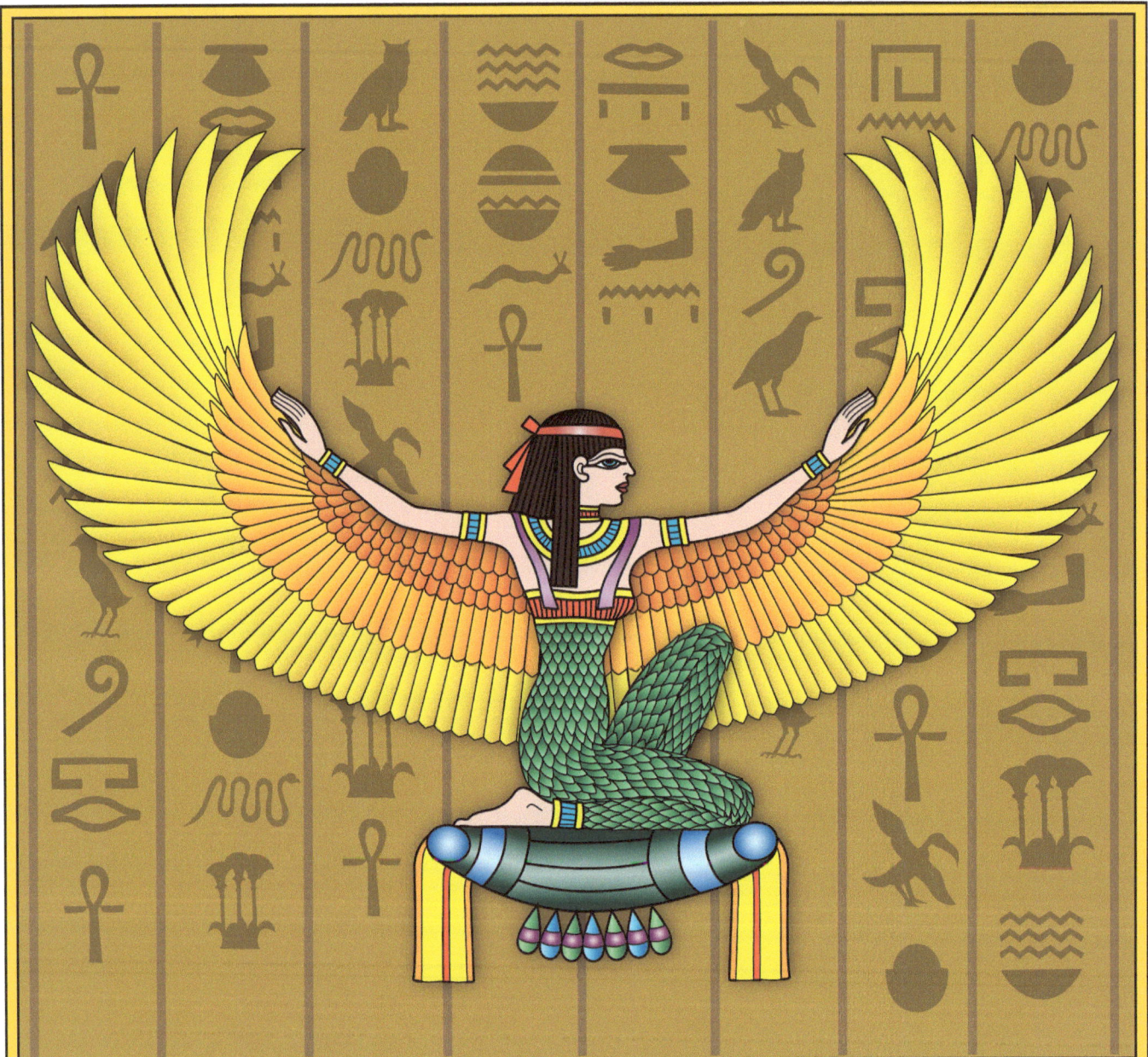

An image of the winged goddess Isis, chased with delicacy and skill beneath
the foot of Tutankhamun's innermost gold coffin. 1332 - 1323 B.C.E.

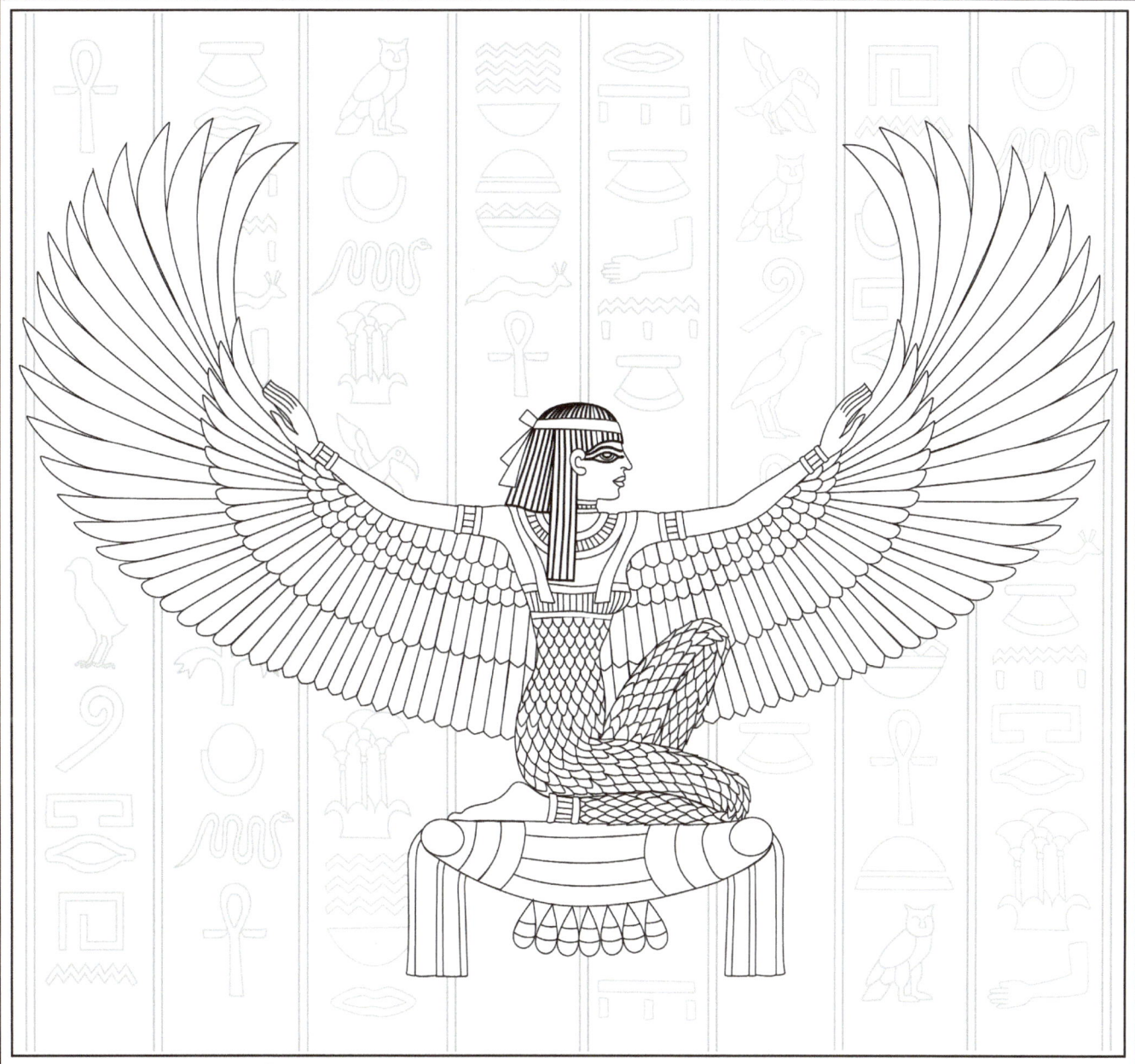

Color the drawing above using your preferred choice of colors.

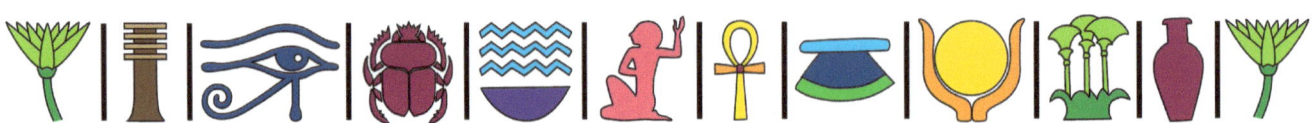

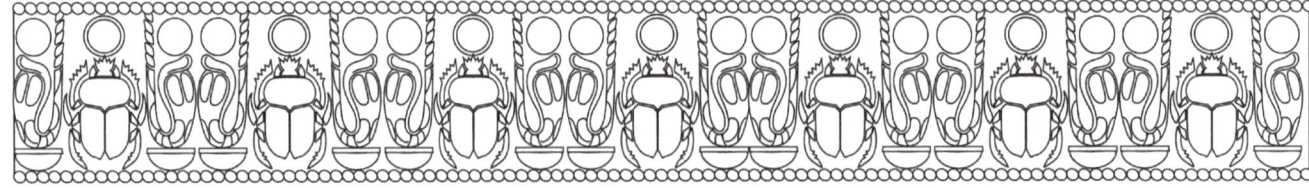

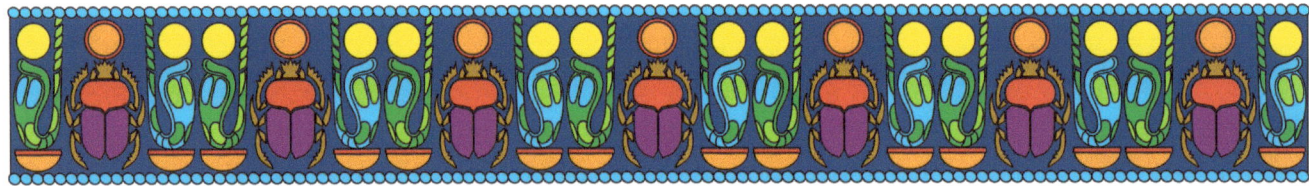

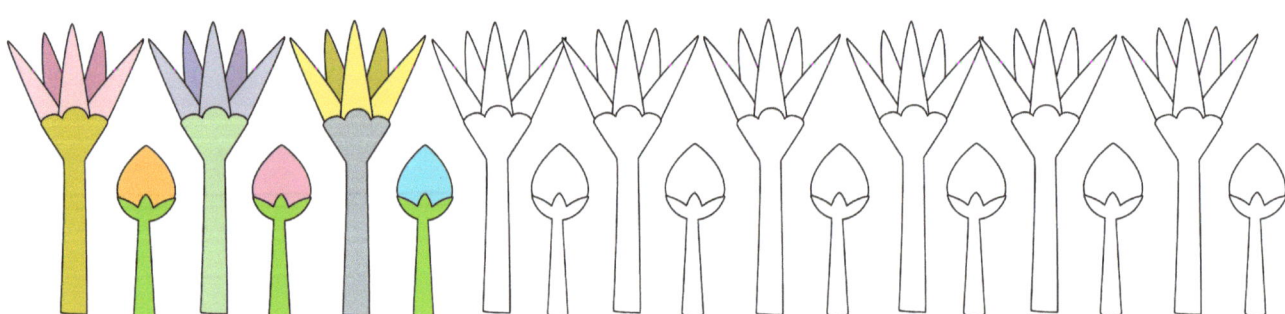

Using these images as examples, create your own piece using the elements found in Egyptian Art.

Egyptian Art

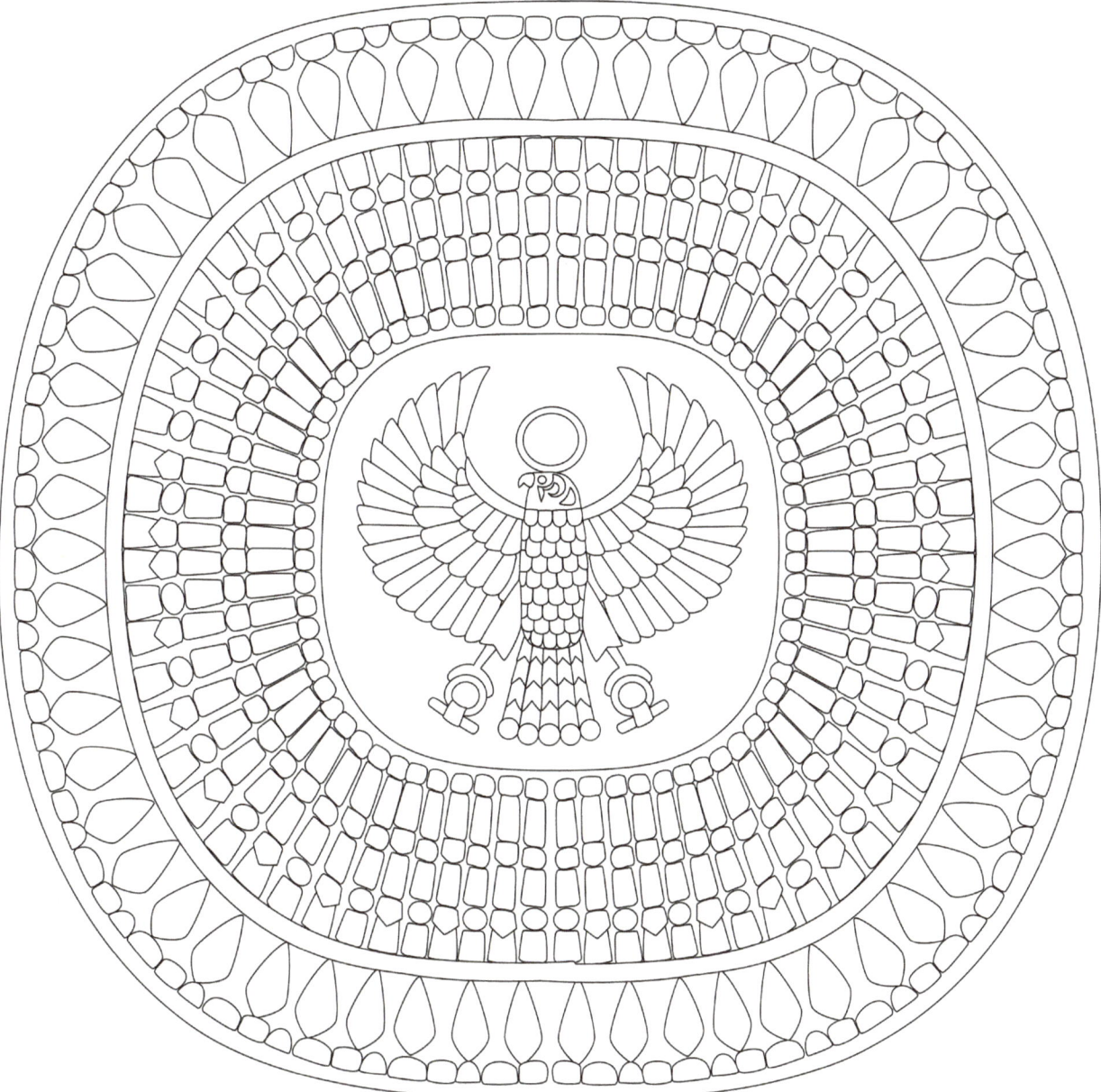

Color the drawings above using your preferred choice of colors.

37

= a synopsis of =

Egyptian art

Ancient Egyptian Civilization produced paintings, sculptures, architecture, potteries and a variety of other forms of art in the Nile Valley from 5000 B.C.E. till 300 C.E. Most of their art consists of static yet formal, as well as abstract, and is overall blocky by nature. Egyptian art reached its peak with their stylized symbolic paintings and sculptures during the reign of over 30 dynasties of the Pharaoh lineage.

Egyptian art forms are characterized by detailed depiction of their gods, people, heroic battles, nature, and their want to provide solace to the afterlife of the deceased. Art was created using a wide range of media such as papyrus drawings to hieroglyphics, and sculptures on sandstone, quartz diorite, and on granite. Egyptian art is an extraordinarily vivid representation of their socioeconomic status and belief system. Their art in unison obeyed the form of representing Pharaohs, gods, man, nature, and the environment that remained for thousands of years.

Ancient Egyptian sculptors used clay, wood, metal, ivory and stone in creating their art. Often sculptors were painted in vivid hues and had two distinctive qualities such as cubic and frontal. Egyptians were exceptionally skilled in creating pottery as well. Symbolism played an important role in establishing a sense of order. Blue represented the Nile and the life; yellow stood for the Sun God and red for power and vitality.

Artists used horizontal and vertical lines to maintain the correct proportions in their work. In order to define the social hierarchy of a situation, figures were drawn to size based on their relative importance. Pharaohs were drawn largest in the paintings, and their greater Gods were drawn larger in scale than the lesser gods. Clear and simple lines combined with simple shapes and flat areas of color helped create a sense of order and balance in the art.

Hieroglyphs may have been there since prehistoric era but Egyptians developed it as a full form of language by 3100 B.C.E., and it lasted till 394 C.E. Hieroglyphics were found everywhere in ancient Egypt, either simply incised in stone or gold, or gleaming with vibrant colors. A brilliant Englishman, Thomas Young, (1773 - 1829) did the first breakthrough and the young French scholar, Jean Francois Champollion, was finally successful in deciphering the Egyptian Hieroglyphics in 1822.

OTHER TITLES IN THIS SERIES

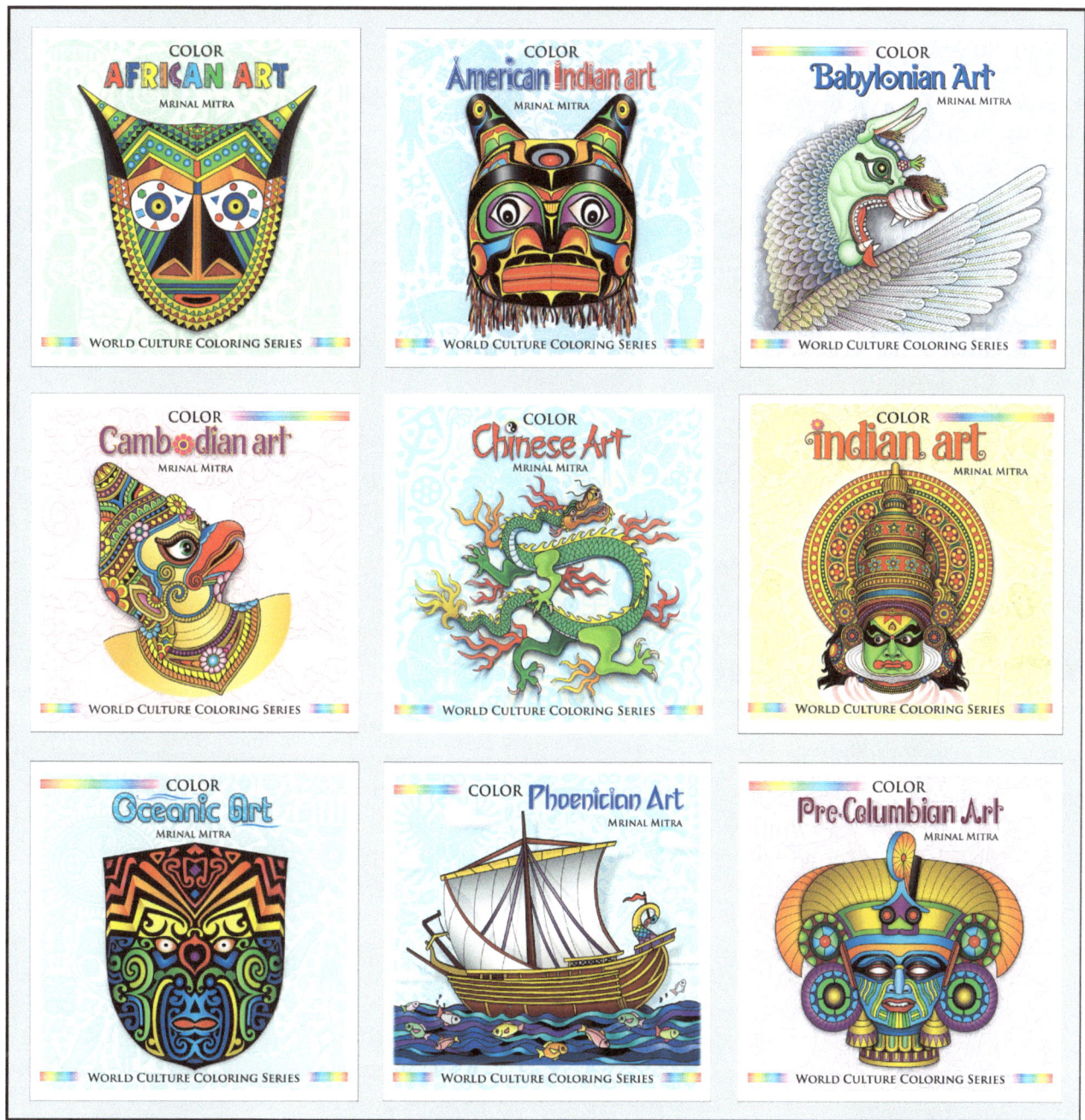

COLOR
AFRICAN ART
MRINAL MITRA
WORLD CULTURE COLORING SERIES

COLOR
American Indian art
MRINAL MITRA
WORLD CULTURE COLORING SERIES

COLOR
Babylonian Art
MRINAL MITRA
WORLD CULTURE COLORING SERIES

COLOR
Cambodian art
MRINAL MITRA
WORLD CULTURE COLORING SERIES

COLOR
Chinese Art
MRINAL MITRA
WORLD CULTURE COLORING SERIES

COLOR
indian art
MRINAL MITRA
WORLD CULTURE COLORING SERIES

COLOR
Oceanic art
MRINAL MITRA
WORLD CULTURE COLORING SERIES

COLOR **Phoenician Art**
MRINAL MITRA
WORLD CULTURE COLORING SERIES

COLOR
Pre-Columbian Art
MRINAL MITRA
WORLD CULTURE COLORING SERIES

AVAILABLE FROM AMAZON.COM, CREATESPACE.COM, AND OTHER RETAIL OUTLETS

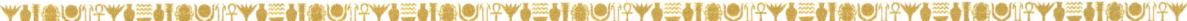

Acknowledgement

First and foremost, this series would not be possible without the number of great historical art found within the different cultural regions around the world.

In addition, we would like to acknowledge the variety of publishing's from all over the world for allowing us to learn about their fascinating ancestral art and culture. With this provided knowledge, we have hoped to have represented the art as splendidly as you have supplied it.

About the Author

Mrinal Mitra has earned a number of prestigious awards, both Indian and International, and received honors for his outstanding illustrations. Some of his recognitions include; The Noma Concours Award, Japan (twice), Illustrators Award, and Children's Choice Award, India, and honors from German Television "Transtel", BRNO- CSSR, TIBI- Iran, and UNICEF, New York.

Many of his talented artworks have been exhibited in several different countries such as; India, Japan, Italy, Czech Republic, Iran, and New Zealand. Mitra has authored, designed and illustrated trade and educational children's books for many Indian as well as Multinational Book Publishers around the globe.

Copyright: Mrinal Mitra, 2014

Printed by CreateSpace, An Amazon.com. Company
Available from Amazon.com, CreateSpace.com, and other retail outlets

For further inquiry please contact Mrinal Mitra at: mitra_mrinal@hotmail.com